Geometry

LARSON
BOSWELL
STIFF

Applying • Reasoning • Measuring

Notetaking Guide

The Notetaking Guide contains a lesson-by-lesson framework that allows students to take notes on and review the main concepts of each lesson in the textbook. Each Notetaking Guide lesson features worked-out examples and Checkpoint exercises. Each example has a number of write-on lines for students to complete, either in class as the example is discussed or at home as part of a review of the lesson. Each chapter concludes with a review of the main vocabulary of the chapter. Upon completion, each chapter of the Notetaking Guide can be used by students to help review for the test on that particular chapter.

McDougal Littell
A HOUGHTON MIFFLIN COMPANY
Evanston, Illinois • Boston • Dallas

ISBN: 0-618-41023-6

456789–VEI–08 07 06 05 04

Contents

Geometry Notetaking Guide

Contents

Contents

Contents

1.1 Patterns and Inductive Reasoning

Goals • Find and describe patterns.
• Use inductive reasoning to make conjectures.

VOCABULARY

Conjecture

Inductive reasoning

Counterexample

Example 1 *Describing a Visual Pattern*

Sketch the next figure in the pattern.

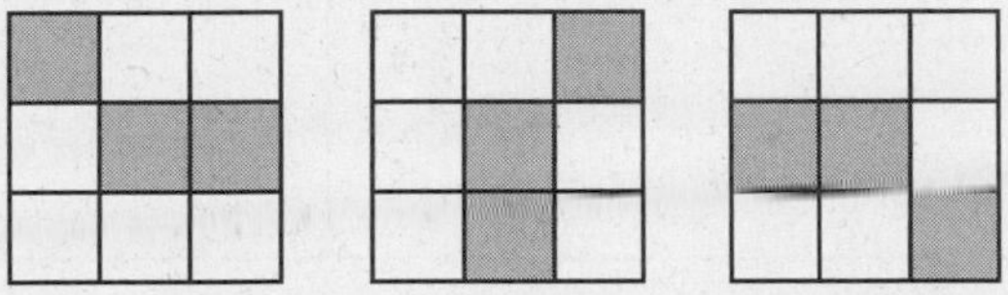

Solution

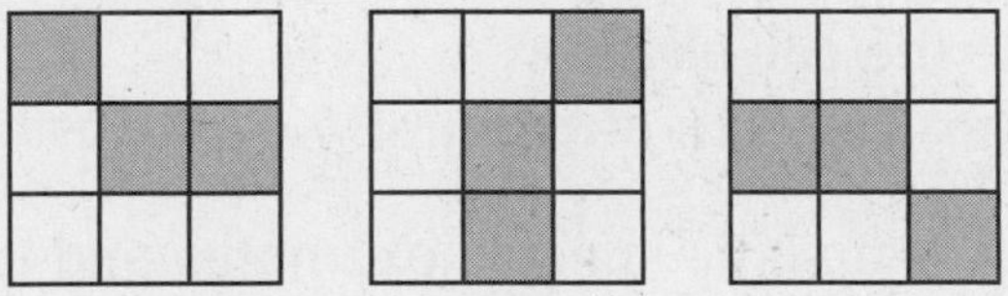

> How does the shading change from one figure to the next? Is the figure rotated?

✓ *Checkpoint* Sketch the next figure in the pattern.

1.

Example 2   *Describing a Number Pattern*

Describe a pattern in the sequence of numbers. Predict the next number.

a. 128, 64, 32, 16, …   **b.** 5, 4, 2, −1, …

Solution

a. Each number is _____ the previous number. The next number is ___.

b. Subtract ___ to get the second number, then subtract ___ to get the third number, then subtract ___ to get the fourth number. To find the fifth number, subtract ___ from the fourth number.

    Answer So, the next number is ____ − ___, or ____.

✔ **Checkpoint** Describe a pattern in the sequence of numbers. Predict the next number.

2. 4, −20, 100, −500, …	**3.** 10, 20, 40, 70, 110, …

Example 3   *Making a Conjecture*

Complete the conjecture.
Conjecture: The sum of the first n even positive integers is ___?___ .

Solution List some specific examples and look for a pattern.

    Examples:

first even integer:	$2 = 1(\underline{})$
sum of first **two** even positive integers:	$2 + 4 = \underline{} = 2(\underline{})$
sum of first **three** even positive integers:	$2 + 4 + 6 = \underline{} = 3(\underline{})$
sum of first **four** even positive integers:	$2 + 4 + 6 + 8 = \underline{} = 4(\underline{})$

Conjecture: The sum of the first n even positive integers is

_____ .

Example 4 *Finding a Counterexample*

Show the conjecture is false by finding a counterexample.

Conjecture: If the difference of two numbers is odd, then the greater of the two numbers must also be odd.

Solution

Counterexample: ___ − ___ = ___

So, the conjecture is _____ .

> Write a difference so that the greater of the two numbers is even.

✔ *Checkpoint* **Complete the following exercises.**

4. Complete the conjecture based on the pattern you observe.

$$1 = 1$$

$$1 + 2 = 3 = \frac{2(2 + 1)}{2}$$

$$1 + 2 + 3 = 6 = \frac{3(3 + 1)}{2}$$

$$1 + 2 + 3 + 4 = 10 = \frac{4(4 + 1)}{2}$$

$$1 + 2 + 3 + 4 + 5 = 15 = \frac{5(5 + 1)}{2}$$

$$1 + 2 + 3 + 4 + 5 + 6 = 21 = \frac{6(6 + 1)}{2}$$

Conjecture: The sum of the first n positive integers

is _____ .

5. Show the conjecture is false by finding a counterexample.

Conjecture: The difference of two negative numbers is always negative.

1.2 Points, Lines, and Planes

Goals • Understand and use the basic undefined terms and defined terms of geometry.
• Sketch the intersections of lines and planes.

VOCABULARY

Point

Line

Plane

Collinear points

Coplanar points

Line segment, Endpoint

Ray, Initial point

Opposite rays

Intersect

Intersection

Example 1 *Naming Collinear and Coplanar Points*

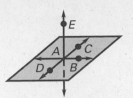

a. Name three points that are collinear.

b. Name three points that are coplanar.

c. Name four points that are not coplanar.

Solution

a. Points ___ , ___ , and ___ lie on the same line, so they are collinear.

b. There are many correct answers. For instance, points ___ , ___ , and ___ lie on the same plane. Also, points ___ , ___ , and ___ are coplanar, although the plane containing them is not drawn.

c. There are many correct answers. For instance, points ___ , ___ , ___ , and ___ do not lie on the same plane.

✔ *Checkpoint* **Complete the following exercises.**

1. Name three points in the diagram that are not collinear.

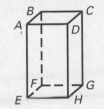

_____

2. Name the point in the diagram that is coplanar with points *A*, *D*, and *E*.

Example 2 *Drawing Lines, Segments, and Rays*

Draw four noncollinear points, *A*, *B*, *C*, and *D*. Then draw $\overline{AB}$, $\overrightarrow{BC}$, $\overleftrightarrow{CD}$, $\overrightarrow{DA}$, and $\overrightarrow{BD}$.

A, *B*, *C*, and *D* are shown.

1. Draw $\overline{AB}$.

2. Draw $\overrightarrow{BC}$.

3. Draw $\overleftrightarrow{CD}$.

4. Draw $\overrightarrow{DA}$.

5. Draw $\overrightarrow{BD}$.

B •

• C

A •

• D

Example 3 *Drawing Opposite Rays*

Draw a line. Label three points on the line and name a pair of opposite rays.

Draw points *X*, *Y*, and *Z* on the given line so that *Y* is between *X* and *Z*.

The opposite rays are _____ and _____.

Example 4 *Sketching Intersections*

Sketch two lines that do not intersect and a line that intersects each of the other lines.

Draw a line that does not intersect the given line.

Then draw a third line that intersects the first two lines. Emphasize the points of intersection.

✔ *Checkpoint* Sketch the figure described.

3. Draw points *A*, *B*, and *C* so that they are not collinear. Then sketch $\overleftrightarrow{BC}$, $\overline{AC}$, and $\overrightarrow{BA}$.	**4.** Sketch two planes that do not intersect and a line that intersects each plane in a point.

1.3 Segments and Their Measures

Goals • Use segment postulates.
• Use the Distance Formula to measure distances.

VOCABULARY

Postulates

Coordinate

Distance

Length

Between

Distance Formula

Congruent segments

POSTULATE 1: RULER POSTULATE

The points on a line can be matched one to one with real numbers. The real number that corresponds to a point is the _____ of the point.

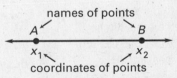

The _____ between points A and B, written as AB, is the absolute value of the difference between the coordinates of A and B.

AB is also called the _____ of $\overline{AB}$.

Example 1   Finding the Distance Between Two Points

Measure the length of the segment to the nearest tenth of a centimeter.

$AB = |\underline{\quad} - \underline{\quad}|$

$= \underline{\quad\quad}$

Answer The length of $\overline{AB}$ is about _____ centimeters.

POSTULATE 2: SEGMENT ADDITION POSTULATE

If B is between A and C, then $AB + BC = AC$. If $AB + BC = AC$, then B is between A and C.

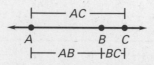

Example 2   Finding Distances on a Map

Reading a Map Use the map to find the distance between the three locations that lie on a line.

Use the scale on the map to find the distance between the library and the stadium and the distance between the stadium and the museum.

> To measure the length of a segment, place an edge of a sheet of paper next to the scale. Mark the scale on the paper and use it to measure the segment.

$LS = \underline{\qquad\qquad}$

$SM = \underline{\qquad\qquad}$

Knowing that the library, stadium, and museum lie on the same line, you can use the Segment Addition Postulate to find the distance between the library and the museum.

$LM = \underline{\quad} + \underline{\quad}$ **Segment Addition Postulate**

$ = \underline{\quad} + \underline{\quad}$ **Substitute for LS and SM.**

$ = \underline{\quad}$ **Simplify.**

Answer The distance between the library and the museum is _____ miles.

THE DISTANCE FORMULA

If $A(x_1, y_1)$ and $B(x_2, y_2)$ are points in a coordinate plane, then the distance between A and B is

$AB = $ _____ .

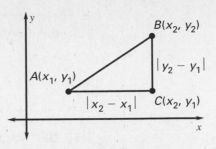

Example 3   *Using the Distance Formula*

Find the lengths of the segments. Tell whether any of the segments have the same length.

Use the Distance Formula.

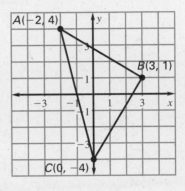

$AB = \sqrt{(\underline{} - (-2))^2 + (\underline{} - \underline{})^2}$

$= \sqrt{\underline{}^2 + (\underline{})^2}$

$= \sqrt{\underline{} + \underline{}}$

$= \underline{}$

$AC = \sqrt{(0 - (\underline{}))^2 + ((\underline{}) - \underline{})^2}$

$= \sqrt{\underline{}^2 + (\underline{})^2}$

$= \sqrt{\underline{} + \underline{}}$

$= \underline{}$

$BC = \sqrt{(\underline{} - 3)^2 + (\underline{} - 1)^2}$

$= \sqrt{(\underline{})^2 + (\underline{})^2}$

$= \sqrt{\underline{} + \underline{}}$

$= \underline{}$

Answer So, _____ and _____ have the same length.

✔ **Checkpoint** Sketch a segment that has the given length.

1. 3.4 centimeters	**2.** 4.2 centimeters

Use the Segment Addition Postulate to find the length.

3. Find *JL*.	**4.** Find *QR*.
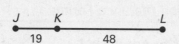	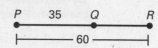

5. Find the lengths of the segments. Tell whether any of the segments have the same length.

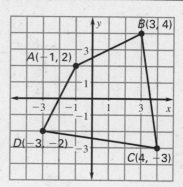

AB = _____   *BC* = _____

CD = _____   · *AD* = _____

_____ and _____ have the same length.

_____ and _____ have the same length.

1.4 Angles and Their Measures

Goals
- Use angle postulates.
- Classify angles as acute, right, obtuse, or straight.

VOCABULARY

Angle

Sides of an angle

Vertex of an angle

Congruent angles

Measure of an angle

Interior of an angle

Exterior of an angle

Acute angle

Right angle

Obtuse angle

Straight angle

Adjacent angles

Example 1 **Naming Angles**

Name the angles in the figure.

There are three different angles.

- _____ or _____
- _____ or _____
- _____ or _____

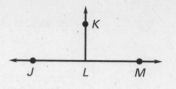

✔ **Checkpoint** Write two names for the angle.

1. 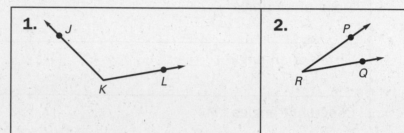	**2.**

POSTULATE 3: PROTRACTOR POSTULATE

Consider a point A on one side of $\overleftrightarrow{OB}$. The rays of the form $\overrightarrow{OA}$ can be matched one to one with the real numbers from 0 to _____.

The measure of _____ is equal to _____

_____ between the real numbers for $\overrightarrow{OA}$ and $\overrightarrow{OB}$.

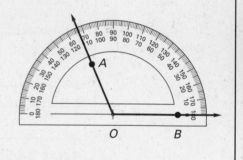

POSTULATE 4: ANGLE ADDITION POSTULATE

If P is in the interior of $\angle RST$, then

_____ + _____ = _____ .

$m\angle RST$
$m\angle RSP$
$m\angle PST$

Example 2 **Calculating Angle Measures**

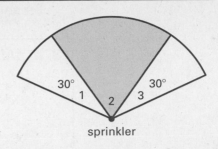

Lawn Care A lawn is watered by a sprinkler that has two fixed spray heads that each spray water in a fan shape. The angle that determines each of the fan shapes is 120°. The shaded area in the diagram shows where the two fan shapes overlap. Find the measure of ∠2.

Solution

$m\angle 1 + m\angle 2 =$ _____	Angle Addition Postulate
_____ $+ m\angle 2 =$ _____	Substitute.
$m\angle 2 =$ _____ $-$ _____	Subtract _____ from each side.
$m\angle 2 =$ _____	Subtract.

Answer So, the measure of ∠2 is _____.

Example 3 **Classifying Angles in a Coordinate Plane**

Measure the angle. Then classify the angle as acute, right, obtuse, or straight.

a. ∠AFD

b. ∠AFE

c. ∠BFD

d. ∠BFC

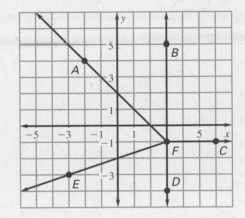

Solution

Use a protractor to measure each angle.

   Measure   **Classification**

a. $m\angle AFD =$ _____   _____

b. $m\angle AFE =$ _____   _____

c. $m\angle BFD =$ _____   _____

d. $m\angle BFC =$ _____   _____

✔ *Checkpoint* Use the Angle Addition Postulate to find the measure of the angle.

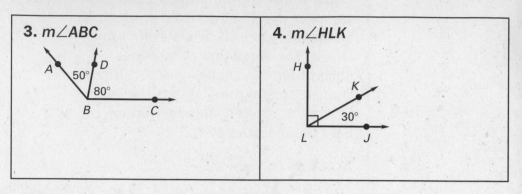

3. *m∠ABC*

4. *m∠HLK*

State whether the angle appears to be *acute*, *right*, *obtuse*, or *straight*. Then estimate its measure.

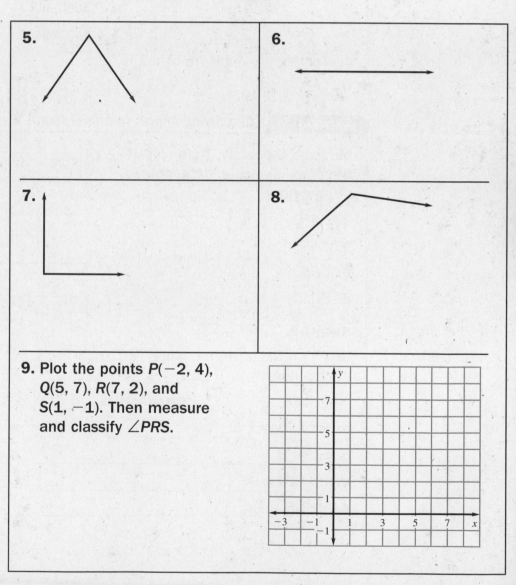

5.

6.

7.

8.

9. Plot the points *P*(−2, 4), *Q*(5, 7), *R*(7, 2), and *S*(1, −1). Then measure and classify ∠*PRS*.

1.5 Segment and Angle Bisectors

Goals • Bisect a segment.
• Bisect an angle.

VOCABULARY

Midpoint

Bisect

Segment bisector

Compass

Straightedge

Construct

Construction

Midpoint Formula

Angle bisector

THE MIDPOINT FORMULA

If $A(x_1, y_1)$ and $B(x_2, y_2)$ are points in a coordinate plane, then the midpoint of $\overline{AB}$ has coordinates

_____

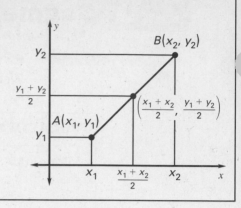

Example 1   *Finding the Coordinates of the Midpoint of a Segment*

Find the coordinates of the midpoint of $\overline{AB}$ with endpoints $A(-3, -4)$ and $B(5, 5)$.

Use the Midpoint Formula.

$$M = \left(\frac{\boxed{} + \boxed{}}{\boxed{}}, \frac{\boxed{} + \boxed{}}{\boxed{}} \right)$$

$$= \left(\underline{}, \underline{} \right)$$

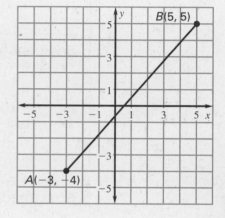

Example 2   *Finding the Coordinates of an Endpoint of a Segment*

The midpoint of $\overline{JK}$ is $M(1, 4)$. One endpoint is $J(-3, 2)$. Find the coordinates of the other endpoint.

Let (x, y) be the coordinates of K. Use the Midpoint Formula to write equations involving x and y.

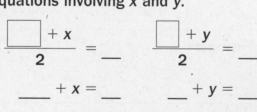

$$\frac{\boxed{} + x}{2} = \underline{} \qquad \frac{\boxed{} + y}{2} = \underline{}$$

$$\underline{} + x = \underline{} \qquad \underline{} + y = \underline{}$$

$$x = \underline{} \qquad y = \underline{}$$

Answer So, the other endpoint of the segment is _____.

✔ Checkpoint Complete the following exercises.

1. Find the coordinates of the midpoint of $\overline{WZ}$. 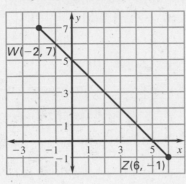	**2.** The midpoint of $\overline{PQ}$ is $M(5, 3)$. Find the coordinates of Q. 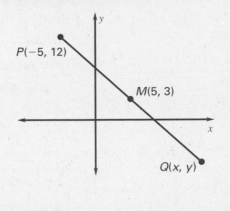

Example 3   *Dividing an Angle Measure in Half*

$\overrightarrow{RT}$ is the angle bisector of $\angle QRS$. Given that $m\angle QRS = 90°$, what are the measures of $\angle QRT$ and $\angle TRS$?

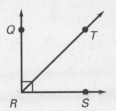

An angle bisector divides an angle into _____ _____, each of which has half the measure of the original angle. So,

$$m\angle QRT = m\angle \_\_\_\_\_ = \underset{\_\_\_\_\_}{} = \_\_\_\_.$$

✔ Checkpoint $\overrightarrow{EG}$ is the angle bisector of $\angle DEF$. Find the two angle measures not given in the diagram.

3.

D   G

52°

E   F

4.

D   G

64°

E   F

Example 4 *Finding the Measure of an Angle*

In the diagram, $\overrightarrow{KM}$ bisects $\angle JKL$. The measures of the two congruent angles are $(2x + 7)°$ and $(4x - 41)°$. Find the measures of $\angle JKM$ and $\angle MKL$.

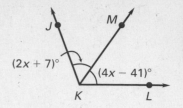

Write an equation, then solve for x.

$m\angle JKM = $ _____	Congruent angles have equal measures.
(_____)° = (_____)°	Substitute given measures.
___ + ___ = ___	Add ___ to each side.
___ = ___	Subtract ___ from each side.
___ = x	Divide each side by ___ .

To find the measure of each congruent angle, substitute ___ for x in one of the expressions.

$(2x + 7)° = (2 \cdot $ ___ $ + 7)°$	Substitute ___ for x.
$= $ ___ °	Simplify.

Answer Each of the congruent angles has a measure of ___ .

✔ **Checkpoint** $\overrightarrow{BD}$ is the angle bisector of $\angle ABC$. Find $m\angle ABD$ and $m\angle DBC$.

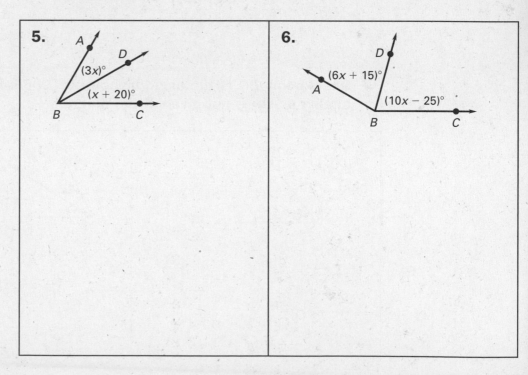

5.

$(3x)°$
$(x + 20)°$

6.

$(6x + 15)°$
$(10x - 25)°$

1.6 Angle Pair Relationships

Goals • Identify vertical angles and linear pairs.
• Identify complementary and supplementary angles.

VOCABULARY

Vertical angles

Linear pair

Complementary angles

Complement

Supplementary angles

Supplement

Example 1   *Finding Angle Measures*

In the flag shown at the right, ∠1 has
a measure of 60°. Find *m*∠2 and *m*∠3.

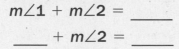

Solution

∠1 and ∠2 are a _____. So, the
sum of their measures is _____.

$m∠1 + m∠2 =$ _____

_____ $+ m∠2 =$ _____

$m∠2 =$ _____

∠1 and ∠3 are _____. So, they are _____ and
have the same _____.

$m∠3 = m∠1 =$ _____

Example 2 *Finding Angle Measures*

Solve for *x* and *y*. Then find the angle measures.

Use the fact that the sum of the measures of angles that form a linear pair is _____.

$$m\angle EDF + m\angle EDH = \underline{\quad}$$

$$(\underline{\qquad})° + (\underline{\qquad})° = \underline{\quad}$$

$$\underline{\quad} = \underline{\quad}$$

$$x = \underline{\quad}$$

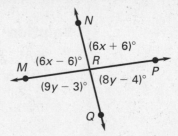

$$m\angle GDF + m\angle GDH = \underline{\quad}$$

$$(\underline{\qquad})° + (\underline{\qquad})° = \underline{\quad}$$

$$\underline{\quad} = \underline{\quad}$$

$$\underline{\quad} = \underline{\quad}$$

$$y = \underline{\quad}$$

Use substitution to find the angle measures.

$$m\angle EDF = (2x + 5)° = (2 \cdot \underline{\quad} + 5)° = \underline{\quad}$$

$$m\angle EDH = (4x - 5)° = (4 \cdot \underline{\quad} - 5)° = \underline{\quad}$$

$$m\angle GDF = (3y + 5)° = (3 \cdot \underline{\quad} + 5)° = \underline{\quad}$$

$$m\angle GDH = (7y - 25)° = (7 \cdot \underline{\quad} - 25)° = \underline{\quad}$$

✔ *Checkpoint* **Complete the following exercises.**

1. The measure of ∠2 is 52°. Find the measures of ∠1, ∠3, and ∠4.	**2.** Solve for *x* and *y*. Then find the angle measures.

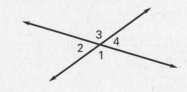

Example 3 *Identifying Angles*

State whether the two angles are *complementary*, *supplementary*, or *neither*.

The angle showing 11:00 has a measure of ____. The angle showing 2:00 has a measure of ____. Because the sum of these two measures is ____, the angles are _____.

Example 4 *Finding Measures of Complements and Supplements*

a. Given that $\angle S$ is a complement of $\angle T$ and $m\angle S = 32°$, find $m\angle T$.

b. Given that $\angle U$ is a supplement of $\angle V$ and $m\angle U = 27°$, find $m\angle V$.

Solution

a. $m\angle T = 90° - \underline{\hspace{1cm}} = 90° - \underline{\hspace{1cm}} = \underline{\hspace{1cm}}$

b. $m\angle V = \underline{\hspace{1cm}} - m\angle U = \underline{\hspace{1cm}} - \underline{\hspace{1cm}} = \underline{\hspace{1cm}}$

✔ *Checkpoint* State whether the two angles are *complementary*, *supplementary*, or *neither*.

3.  	4.
5. $\angle M$ is a complement of $\angle N$ and $m\angle M = 63°$. Find $m\angle N$.	6. $\angle C$ is a supplement of $\angle D$ and $m\angle C = 109°$. Find $m\angle D$.

1.7 Introduction to Perimeter, Circumference, and Area

Goals • Find the perimeter and area of common plane figures.
• Use a general problem-solving plan.

PERIMETER, CIRCUMFERENCE, AND AREA FORMULAS

Formulas for the perimeter P, area A, and circumference C of some common plane figures are given below.

Square
side length s

$P =$ ____

$A =$ ____

Rectangle
length ℓ and width w

$P =$ _____

$A =$ ____

Triangle
side lengths a, b,
and c, base b,
and height h

$P =$ _____

$A =$
_____

Circle
radius r

$C =$ ____

$A =$ ____

Pi (π) is the ratio of the circle's circumference to its diameter.

Example 1   Finding the Perimeter and Area of a Rectangle

Find the perimeter and area of the rectangle.

Use the formulas for the perimeter and area of a rectangle.

$P = 2\ell + 2w$

$= 2 \cdot$ ___ $+ 2 \cdot$ ___

$=$ ___ $+$ ___

$=$ ___

$A = \ell w$

$=$ ___ $\cdot$ ___

$=$ ___

8 m

13 m

Answer The perimeter is ____ meters and the area is ____ square meters.

Example 2   *Finding the Area and Circumference of a Circle*

Find the radius, circumference, and area of the circle. Use 3.14 as an approximation for π.

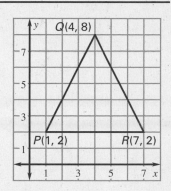

12 in.

From the diagram, you can see that the diameter of the circle is 12 inches. The radius is one half of the diameter.

$$r = \frac{1}{2}(\underline{\quad}) = \underline{\quad} \text{ in.}$$

Use the formulas for the circumference and area of a circle.

$$C = 2\pi r \approx 2(\underline{\quad\quad})(\underline{\quad}) \approx \underline{\quad\quad\quad} \text{ in.}$$
$$A = \pi r^2 \approx (\underline{\quad\quad})(\underline{\quad})^2 \approx \underline{\quad\quad\quad} \text{ in.}^2$$

Example 3   *Finding Measurements of a Triangle in a Coordinate Plane*

Find the area and perimeter of the triangle shown in the coordinate plane.

Draw the height from *Q* to side $\overline{PR}$. Label the point where the height meets $\overline{PR}$ as *S*. Point *S* has the coordinates (__, __).

base: $PR = \underline{\quad} - 1 = \underline{\quad}$

height: $QS = 8 - \underline{\quad} = \underline{\quad}$

$$A = \frac{1}{2}bh = \frac{1}{2}(\underline{\quad})(\underline{\quad})$$
$$= \underline{\quad} \text{ square units}$$

To find the perimeter, use the Distance Formula.

$$PQ = \sqrt{(\underline{\quad} - 1)^2 + (8 - \underline{\quad})^2}$$
$$= \sqrt{\underline{\quad}^2 + \underline{\quad}^2}$$
$$= \underline{\quad\quad} = \underline{\quad\quad} \text{ units}$$

$$QR = \sqrt{(7 - \underline{\quad})^2 + (\underline{\quad} - 8)^2}$$
$$= \sqrt{\underline{\quad}^2 + (\underline{\quad})^2}$$
$$= \underline{\quad\quad} = \underline{\quad\quad} \text{ units}$$

The perimeter is $PQ + QR + PR = (\underline{\quad\quad} + \underline{\quad\quad} + \underline{\quad})$, or $\underline{\quad} + \underline{\quad\quad}$, units.

> When simplifying radicals, remember that if *a* and *b* are positive numbers, then $\sqrt{ab} = \sqrt{a} \cdot \sqrt{b}$.

Coordinate plane shows: Q(4, 8), P(1, 2), R(7, 2); axis labels 7, 5, 3, 1 on y-axis and 1, 3, 5, 7 x on x-axis.

1.

12 mm

12 mm

2.

15 in.   25 in.

20 in.

3.

22 cm

4. Find the area and the perimeter of the triangle defined by J(1, 4), K(9, 4), and L(4, 0).

A PROBLEM-SOLVING PLAN

1. Ask yourself what you need to solve the problem. Write a _____ or _____ that will help you find what you need to know.

2. _____ on or near your sketch.

3. Use labels and facts to _____ _____ , or other results you may need.

4. _____ to link the facts, using a proof or other written argument.

5. Write a _____ that answers the original problem. _____ that your reasoning is correct.

Example 4   *Using the Area of a Triangle*

> It might be helpful to draw a sketch of the kite and label the given dimensions. Remember to always check your answers.

Kite Design You are designing a triangular kite with a height of 64 inches and an area of 4096 square inches. What is the base of the kite?

Solution

Verbal Model	$\boxed{\text{Area of kite}}$ $= \dfrac{1}{2} \cdot$ $\boxed{\text{Base of kite}}$ $\cdot$ $\boxed{\text{Height of kite}}$

Labels   Area of kite = _____   (square inches)

             _____ = b (inches)

             _____ = 64   (inches)

Reasoning   _____ $= \dfrac{1}{2}($___$)$___   Write equation for kite area.

             _____ $=$ ___ $\cdot$ ___   Simplify.

             _____ $= b$ Divide each side by ____ .

Answer The base of the kite is _____ inches.

✔ *Checkpoint* Complete the following exercise.

---

5. You need to buy mulch for a rectangular flower garden. The garden is 6 feet wide and 12 feet long. One bag of mulch will cover 8 square feet. How many bags of mulch should you buy?

Words to Review

Give an example of the vocabulary word.

Conjecture	Point, line, plane
Segment	Ray
Opposite rays	Postulate
Length of a segment	Congruent segments
Angle	Congruent angles

Measure of an angle	Acute angle
Right angle	**Obtuse angle**
Straight angle	**Midpoint**
Segment bisector	**Angle bisector**

Vertical angles	Linear pair
Complementary angles	Supplementary angles

Review your notes and Chapter 1 by using the Chapter Review on pages 60–62 of your textbook.

Conditional Statements

Goals • Recognize and analyze a conditional statement.
• Write postulates about points, lines, and planes using conditional statements.

VOCABULARY

Conditional statement

If-then form

Hypothesis

Conclusion

Converse

Negation

Inverse

Contrapositive

Equivalent statements

Example 1 Rewriting in If-Then Form

Rewrite the conditional statement in *if-then* form.

a. Three points are coplanar if they lie on the same plane.

b. Water freezes at temperatures below 32°F.

c. An even number is divisible by 2.

Solution

a. If _____ , then _____

_____ .

b. If _____ , then _____ .

c. If _____ , then _____ .

Example 2 Writing an Inverse, Converse, and Contrapositive

Write the (a) inverse, (b) converse, and (c) contrapositive of the following statement.

If the sun is shining, then we are not watching TV.

Solution

a. Inverse: _____ .

b. Converse: _____ .

c. Contrapositive: _____

_____ .

✔ *Checkpoint* Write the (a) inverse, (b) converse, and (c) contrapositive of the conditional statement.

1. If my allowance increases, then I can save more money.

POINT, LINE, AND PLANE POSTULATES

Postulate 5   Through any two points there exists exactly one

_____.

Postulate 6   A line contains at least two _____.

Postulate 7   If two lines intersect, then their intersection is

_____.

Postulate 8   Through any three _____ points there exists
exactly one plane.

Postulate 9   A plane contains at least three _____
points.

Postulate 10   If two points lie in a plane, then the line containing
them _____.

Postulate 11   If two planes intersect, then their intersection is a

_____.

Example 3   *Using Postulates and Counterexamples*

Decide whether the statement is *true* or *false*. If it is false, give a
counterexample.

a. A point can lie on more than two lines.

b. Three lines can intersect at no more than three distinct points.

c. If two lines are coplanar, then they intersect.

Solution

a. In the diagram at the right, point *P* is the
_____ of line *k*, line *m*, and line *n*. So,
it is _____ that a point can lie on more than
two lines.

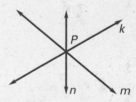

b. In the diagram at the right, line *k* and line *m*
intersect at point ___, line ___ and line ___
intersect at point *Q*, and line ___ and line *n*
intersect at point ___. There are no more
possible intersections. So, it is _____ that
three lines can intersect at no more than
three distinct points.

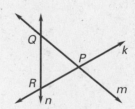

c. In the diagram at the right, line *m* and line *n*
are _____, but they do not _____.
So, it is _____ that if two lines are coplanar,
then they intersect.

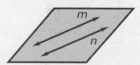

2.2 Definitions and Biconditional Statements

Goals • Recognize and use definitions.
• Recognize and use biconditional statements.

VOCABULARY

Perpendicular lines

Line perpendicular to a plane

Biconditional statement

Example 1 *Using Definitions*

Decide whether each statement about the diagram is true. Explain your answer using the definitions you have learned.

a. $\angle KLJ$ and $\angle KJL$ are complementary.

b. $\overleftrightarrow{KL}$ and $\overleftrightarrow{LJ}$ are perpendicular.

c. $\angle MKJ$ is a right angle.

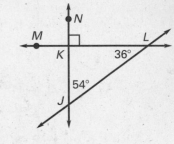

Solution

a. This statement is _____ . Two angles are complementary if the sum of their measures is _____ . $m\angle KLJ + m\angle KJL =$ _____ , so the angles are _____ .

b. This statement is _____ . $\overleftrightarrow{KL}$ and $\overleftrightarrow{LJ}$ do not intersect to form a _____ . So, the lines are _____ .

c. This statement is _____ . $\angle MKJ$ and $\angle NKL$ are _____ angles. $\angle NKL$ is a _____ . Because _____ angles are congruent, $\angle MKJ$ is a _____ .

✔ Checkpoint Use the diagram in Example 1 to decide whether the statement is true. Explain your answer using the definitions you have learned.

1. ∠*KJL* is an acute angle.	2. Point *N* is in the interior of ∠*KLJ*.

Example 2   *Rewriting a Biconditional Statement*

Rewrite the following biconditional statement as a conditional statement and its converse.

An angle is a straight angle if and only if its measure is 180°.

Conditional statement: If _____, then _____.

Converse: If _____, then _____.

Example 3   *Analyzing a Biconditional Statement*

Consider the following statement: $x = 2$ if and only if $3x + 5x = 10x - 2x$.

a. Is this a biconditional statement?   **b.** Is the statement true?

Solution

a. The statement is biconditional because it contains the phrase _____.

b. The statement can be rewritten as the following statement and its converse.

Conditional statement: If _____, then _____.
Converse: If _____, then _____.

The first statement is _____. The second statement is _____. So, the biconditional statement is _____.

> Are there any values other than $x = 2$ that make the equation true?

Example 4   *Writing a Biconditional Statement*

Each of the following statements is true. Write the converse of each statement and decide whether the converse is *true* or *false*. If the converse is true, combine it with the original statement to form a true biconditional statement. If the converse is false, state a counterexample.

a. If $\sqrt{x} = 1$, then $x = 1$.

b. If two angles are vertical angles, then they are congruent.

Solution

a. Converse: _____ . The converse is _____ .

Biconditional statement: _____

b. Converse: _____

_____

_____ . The converse is _____ . As a

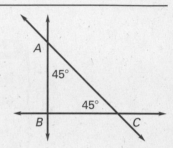

_____ , consider the figure

at the right. $\angle$ _____ and $\angle$ _____ are

congruent, but they are not _____

_____ .

✔ *Checkpoint* **Complete the following exercises.**

3. Rewrite the following biconditional statement as a conditional statement and its converse.

Two angles are supplementary if and only if the sum of their measures is 180°.

4. Consider the following statement: Two segments are congruent if and only if they have the same length.

a. Is the statement biconditional?

b. Is the statement *true* or *false*?

2.3 Deductive Reasoning

Goals • Use symbolic notation to represent logical statements.
• Form conclusions by applying the laws of logic to true statements.

VOCABULARY

Logical argument

Example 1 *Using Symbolic Notation*

Let p be "the value of x is 7" and let q be "x is less than 10."

a. Write $p \rightarrow q$ in words.

b. Write $q \rightarrow p$ in words.

c. Decide whether the biconditional statement $p \leftrightarrow q$ is true.

Solution

a. If _____ , then _____ .

b. If _____ , then _____ .

c. The conditional statement in part (a) is _____ . The converse in part (b) is _____ . So, the biconditional statement $p \leftrightarrow q$ is _____ .

Example 2 *Writing an Inverse and a Contrapositive*

Let p be "my favorite TV show is on" and let q be "it is 8:00 P.M."

a. Write the contrapositive of $p \rightarrow q$.

b. Write the inverse of $p \rightarrow q$.

Solution

a. Contrapositive: $\sim q \rightarrow$ _____
If _____ , then _____ .

b. Inverse: $\sim p \rightarrow$ _____
If _____ , then _____ .

LAW OF DETACHMENT

If $p \rightarrow q$ is a true conditional statement and p is true, then
_____ .

Example 3 *Using the Law of Detachment*

State whether the argument is valid.

a. If Roger gets a part-time job, then he will buy a new bicycle. Roger buys a new bicycle. So, Roger got a part-time job.

b. If two angles are vertical angles, then they are congruent. $\angle 1$ and $\angle 2$ are vertical angles. So, $\angle 1$ and $\angle 2$ are congruent.

Solution

a. This logical argument implies that because Roger bought a new bicycle, he _____ .

The argument is _____ use of the Law of Detachment.

b. The statement $p \rightarrow q$ is _____ and the hypothesis p is _____ . So, you can conclude that the conclusion q is _____ .

The argument is _____ use of the Law of Detachment.

✔ *Checkpoint* In Checkpoint Exercises 1–4, let p be "the stereo is playing" and let q be "I am wearing headphones."

1. Write $p \rightarrow q$.	**2.** Write $q \rightarrow p$.
3. Write $\sim q \rightarrow \sim p$.	**4.** Write $\sim p \rightarrow \sim q$.

5. State whether the following argument is valid. If two adjacent angles form a straight angle, then the angles are supplementary. $\angle 1$ and $\angle 2$ are supplementary. So, you can conclude that $\angle 1$ and $\angle 2$ are adjacent.

LAW OF SYLLOGISM

If $p \rightarrow q$ and $q \rightarrow r$ are true conditional statements, then _____.

Example 4   Using the Law of Syllogism

Write some conditional statements that can be made from the following true statements using the Law of Syllogism.

1. If a cat is the largest of all cats, then it can weigh 650 pounds.

2. If a cat lives in a pride, then it is a lion.

3. If a cat weighs 650 pounds, then it is a tiger.

4. If a cat is a tiger, then it hunts alone.

5. If a cat is a lion, then it can weigh 400 pounds.

Solution

Here are three conditional statements that use the Law of Syllogism.

a. If a cat lives in a pride, then _____.

b. If _____, then it is a tiger.

c. If a cat is the largest of all cats, then _____.

✔ *Checkpoint* **Complete the following exercise.**

6. Write two conditional statements that can be made from the following true statements using the Law of Syllogism.

a. If an elephant lives in India or Southeast Asia, then the elephant is an Indian elephant.

b. If an elephant is an African elephant, then it can weigh up to 8 tons.

c. If an elephant is an Indian elephant, then it can weigh up to 3.5 tons.

d. If an elephant lives in Africa, then it is an African elephant.

2.4 Reasoning with Properties from Algebra

Goals • Use properties from algebra.
• Use properties of length and measure to justify segment and angle relationships.

ALGEBRAIC PROPERTIES OF EQUALITY

Let a, b, and c be real numbers.

Addition Property   If $a = b$, then _____.

Subtraction Property   If $a = b$, then _____.

Multiplication Property If $a = b$, then _____.

Division Property   If $a = b$ and $c \neq 0$, then _____.

Reflexive Property   For any real number a, _____.

Symmetric Property   If $a = b$, then _____.

Transitive Property   If $a = b$ and $b = c$, then _____.

Substitution Property   If $a = b$, then _____

_____.

Example 1   *Writing Reasons*

Solve $-2x + 1 = 56 - 3x$ and write a reason for each step.

$-2x + 1 = 56 - 3x$	Given
___ $+ 1 = 56$	_____
$x =$ ___	_____

✔ *Checkpoint* Solve the equation. Write a reason for each step.

1. $12x - 3(x + 7) = 8x$

Example 2 *Using Properties in Real Life*

Science The Fahrenheit and Celsius temperature scales are related by the formula $F = \dfrac{9}{5}C + 32$, where F represents degrees Fahrenheit and C represents degrees Celsius.

a. Solve the formula for C and write a reason for each step.

b. Use the result to find the Celsius temperatures that correspond to the following Fahrenheit temperatures: 5°F, 32°F, 95°F, 140°F, 212°F. How does the Celsius temperature change as the Fahrenheit temperature changes?

Solution

a.
$$F = \frac{9}{5}C + 32 \qquad \text{Given}$$

$$\underline{\hspace{2cm}} = \frac{9}{5}C \qquad \text{Subtraction property of equality}$$

$$\underline{\hspace{2cm}} = C \qquad \text{Multiplication property of equality}$$

b. Use substitution to find the Celsius temperature that corresponds to 5°F.

$$\frac{5}{9}(F - 32) \quad C \qquad \text{Given}$$

$$\frac{5}{9}(\underline{\hspace{1cm}} - 32) = C \qquad \text{Substitution property of equality}$$

$$\underline{\hspace{1.5cm}} = C \qquad \text{Simplify.}$$

Find the other corresponding temperatures using the same method.

Temperature (°F)	5	32	95	140	212
Temperature (°C)					

From the table, you can see that the Celsius temperature _____ as the Fahrenheit temperature _____.

PROPERTIES OF EQUALITY

	Segment Length	Angle Measure
Reflexive	For any segment AB, _____ .	For any angle A, _____ .
Symmetric	If $AB = CD$, then _____ .	If $m\angle A = m\angle B$, then _____ .
Transitive	If $AB = CD$ and $CD = EF$, then _____ .	If $m\angle A = m\angle B$ and $m\angle B = m\angle C$, then _____ .

Example 3   *Using Properties of Measure*

Use the information at the right to find $m\angle 1$.

$$m\angle 1 + m\angle 2 + m\angle 3 + m\angle 4 = 360°$$
$$m\angle 2 + m\angle 3 = m\angle 4$$
$$m\angle 1 = m\angle 4$$

Solution

$m\angle 1 + m\angle 2 + m\angle 3 + m\angle 4 = $ _____	Given
$m\angle 2 + m\angle 3 = $ _____	Given
$m\angle 1 = $ _____	Given
_____ + _____ + _____ $= 360°$	Substitution property of equality
$3($_____$) = 360°$	Simplify.
_____ $=$ _____	Division property of equality
$m\angle 1 = $ _____	Transitive property of equality

✔ *Checkpoint* **Complete the following exercise.**

2. In the diagram at the right, B is the midpoint of $\overline{AC}$ and C is the midpoint of $\overline{BD}$. Show that $AB = CD$.

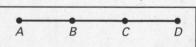

2.5 Proving Statements about Segments

Goals • Justify statements about congruent segments.
• Write reasons for steps in a proof.

VOCABULARY

Theorem

Two-column proof

Paragraph proof

THEOREM 2.1 PROPERTIES OF SEGMENT CONGRUENCE

Reflexive   For any segment AB, _____ .

Symmetric   If $\overline{AB} \cong \overline{CD}$, then _____ .

Transitive   If $\overline{AB} \cong \overline{CD}$, and $\overline{CD} \cong \overline{EF}$, then _____ .

Example 1   *Transitive Property of Segment Congruence*

You can prove the Transitive Property of Segment Congruence as follows.

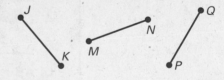

Given: $\overline{JK} \cong \overline{MN}$, $\overline{MN} \cong \overline{PQ}$
Prove: $\overline{JK} \cong \overline{PQ}$

Statements	Reasons
1. $\overline{JK} \cong \overline{MN}$, $\overline{MN} \cong \overline{PQ}$	1. _____
2. $JK = MN$, $MN = PQ$	2. _____
3. _____	3. Transitive property of equality
4. $\overline{JK} \cong \overline{PQ}$	4. Definition of congruent segments

Example 2   *Using Congruence*

Use the diagram and the given information
to complete the proof.

Given: $\overline{PQ} \cong \overline{RS}$, $\overline{PQ} \cong \overline{QR}$, $\overline{PS} \cong \overline{RS}$

Prove: $\overline{PS} \cong \overline{QR}$

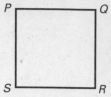

Statements	Reasons
1. $\overline{PQ} \cong \overline{RS}$	1. Given
2. $\overline{PQ} \cong \overline{QR}$	2. _____
3. $\overline{RS} \cong \overline{QR}$	3. Transitive Property of Congruence
4. $\overline{PS} \cong \overline{RS}$	4. _____
5. $\overline{PS} \cong \overline{QR}$	5. Transitive Property of Congruence

Example 3   *Using Segment Relationships*

In the diagram, $AC = CE$ and $AB = DE$.
Show that C is the midpoint of $\overline{BD}$.

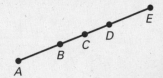

Solution

Given: _____

Prove: _____ .

Statements	Reasons
1. $AC = CE$	1. _____
2. $AB + BC = AC$	2. _____
3. _____	3. Transitive Property of Equality
4. $CD + DE = CE$	4. _____
5. _____	5. Transitive Property of Equality
6. $AB = DE$	6. _____
7. $AB + BC = CD + AB$	7. _____ _____
8. _____	8. Subtraction Property of Equality
9. _____	9. Definition of congruent segments
10. C is the midpoint of $\overline{BD}$.	10. _____

1. In the diagram, $AB = DE$ and $BC = CD$.
Complete the proof to show that C is
the midpoint of $\overline{AE}$.

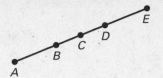

Given: _____

Prove: _____ .

Statements	Reasons
1. $AB = DE$	**1.** _____
2. $AB + BC = DE + BC$	**2.** _____ _____
3. _____	**3.** Given
4. $AB + BC = DE + CD$	**4.** _____ _____
5. $AB + BC = AC$	**5.** _____ _____
6. _____	**6.** Transitive Property of Equality
7. _____	**7.** Segment Addition Postulate
8. _____	**8.** Transitive Property of Equality
9. _____	**9.** Definition of congruent segments
10. C is the midpoint of $\overline{AE}$.	**10.** _____

2.6 Proving Statements about Angles

• Use angle congruence properties.
• Prove properties about special pairs of angles.

THEOREM 2.2 PROPERTIES OF ANGLE CONGRUENCE

Angle congruence is reflexive, symmetric, and transitive.

Reflexive For any angle A, _____.

Symmetric If $\angle A \cong \angle B$, then _____.

Transitive If $\angle A \cong \angle B$ and $\angle B \cong \angle C$, then _____.

Example 1 *Using the Transitive Property*

In the diagram at the right, $\angle 1 \cong \angle 5$, $\angle 5 \cong \angle 3$, and $m\angle 1 = 103°$. What is the measure of $\angle 3$? Explain your reasoning.

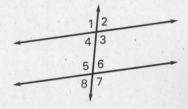

Solution

Because $\angle 1 \cong \angle 5$ and $\angle 5 \cong \angle 3$, you can use the _____ _____ to conclude that _____.

Because congruent angles have the same measure, you can conclude that $m\angle 3 = m\angle 1 =$ _____.

Answer The measure of $\angle 3$ is _____.

✓ *Checkpoint* Use the diagram from Example 1.

1. Given that $\angle 4 \cong \angle 6$, $\angle 6 \cong \angle 8$, and $m\angle 8 = 77°$, what is the measure of $\angle 4$? Explain your reasoning.

THEOREM 2.3 RIGHT ANGLE CONGRUENCE THEOREM

All right angles are _____ .

THEOREM 2.4 CONGRUENT SUPPLEMENTS THEOREM

If two angles are supplementary to the
same angle (or to congruent angles),
then they are _____ .

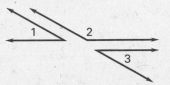

If $m\angle 1 + m\angle 2 =$ _____ and
$m\angle 2 + m\angle 3 =$ _____ , then _____ .

THEOREM 2.5 CONGRUENT COMPLEMENTS THEOREM

If two angles are complementary to the
same angle (or to congruent angles), then
the two angles are _____ .

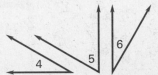

If $m\angle 4 + m\angle 5 =$ _____ and
$m\angle 5 + m\angle 6 =$ _____ , then _____ .

Example 2 *Proving Theorem 2.5*

Given: $\angle 1$ and $\angle 2$ are complements,
  $\angle 3$ and $\angle 4$ are complements,
  $\angle 2 \cong \angle 4$
Prove: $\angle 1 \cong \angle 3$

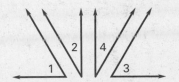

Statements	Reasons
1. $\angle 1$ and $\angle 2$ are complements, $\angle 3$ and $\angle 4$ are complements, $\angle 2 \cong \angle 4$	1. _____
2. $m\angle 1 + m\angle 2 = 90°$, $m\angle 3 + m\angle 4 = 90°$	2. _____
3. _____	3. Transitive property of equality
4. $m\angle 2 = m\angle 4$	4. _____
5. _____	5. Substitution property of equality
6. _____	6. Subtraction property of equality
7. $\angle 1 \cong \angle 3$	7. _____

POSTULATE 12 LINEAR PAIR POSTULATE

If two angles form a linear pair, then
they are _____.

$m\angle 1 + m\angle 2 =$ _____

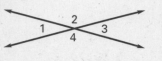

THEOREM 2.6 VERTICAL ANGLES THEOREM

Vertical angles are _____.

$\angle 1 \cong$ _____ and _____ $\cong \angle 4$

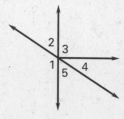

Example 3   *Using Linear Pairs and Vertical Angles*

In the diagram, $\angle 3$ is a right angle and
$m\angle 5 = 57°$. Find the measures of $\angle 1$, $\angle 2$, $\angle 3$,
and $\angle 4$.

Solution

By the definition of a right angle, $m\angle 3 =$ _____.

$\angle 2$ and $\angle 5$ are _____ and $m\angle 5 = 57°$, so $m\angle 2 =$ _____.

$\angle 1$ and $\angle 5$ form a _____, so $m\angle 1 + m\angle 5 =$ _____. When
you substitute _____ for $m\angle 5$ and solve for $m\angle 1$, the result is
$m\angle 1 =$ _____.

$\angle 4$ and $\angle 5$ are _____, so $m\angle 4 + m\angle 5 =$ _____. When
you substitute _____ for $m\angle 5$ and solve for $m\angle 4$, the result is
$m\angle 4 =$ _____.

✔ *Checkpoint* Complete the following exercises.

2. Find $m\angle 1$ and $m\angle 2$. 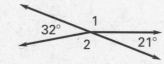	3. Find the measure of each angle. 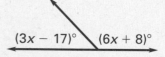

Words to Review

Give an example of the vocabulary word.

Conditional statement	If-then form
Hypothesis	Conclusion
Converse	Negation
Inverse	Contrapositive
Equivalent statement	Perpendicular lines
Line perpendicular to a plane	Biconditional statement

Logical argument	Law of Detachment
Law of Syllogism	Theorem
Two-column proof	Paragraph proof

Review your notes and Chapter 2 by using the Chapter Review on pages 118–120 of your textbook.

3.1 Lines and Angles

Goals • Identify relationships between lines.
• Identify angles formed by transversals.

VOCABULARY

Parallel lines

Skew lines

Parallel planes

Transversal

Corresponding angles

Alternate exterior angles

Alternate interior angles

Consecutive interior angles

Same side interior angles

Example 1 *Identifying Relationships in Space*

Think of each segment in the diagram as part of a line. Which of the lines appear to fit the description?

a. parallel to $\overleftrightarrow{AG}$ and contains C

b. perpendicular to $\overleftrightarrow{AG}$ and contains B

c. skew to $\overleftrightarrow{AG}$ and contains C

d. Name the plane that contains C and appears to be parallel to plane *AFL*.

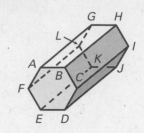

Solution

a. There are _____ lines that are parallel to $\overleftrightarrow{AG}$, but only _____ passes through C and is parallel to $\overleftrightarrow{AG}$.

b. There are _____ lines that are perpendicular to $\overleftrightarrow{AG}$, but only _____ passes through B and is perpendicular to $\overleftrightarrow{AG}$.

c. There are _____ lines that are skew to $\overleftrightarrow{AG}$, but only _____ and _____ pass through C and are skew to $\overleftrightarrow{AG}$.

d. The plane _____ contains C and is parallel to plane *AFL*.

✔ **Checkpoint** Think of each segment in the diagram as part of a line. Which of the lines appear to fit the description?

1. parallel to $\overleftrightarrow{PQ}$ and contains S

2. perpendicular to $\overleftrightarrow{PQ}$ and contains S

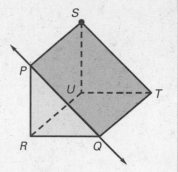

3. skew to $\overleftrightarrow{PQ}$ and contains S

4. Name the plane that contains S and appears to be parallel to plane *PQR*.

POSTULATE 13: PARALLEL POSTULATE

If there is a line and a point not on the line, then there is _____ line through the point parallel to the given line.

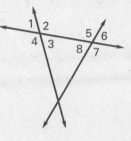

There is _____ line through *P* parallel to *l*.

POSTULATE 14: PERPENDICULAR POSTULATE

If there is a line and a point not on the line, then there is _____ line through the point perpendicular to the given line.

There is _____ line through *P* perpendicular to *l*.

Example 2 *Identifying Angle Relationships*

List all pairs of angles that fit the description.

a. corresponding   **b.** alternate exterior

c. alternate interior   **d.** consecutive interior

Solution

a. ∠1 and ____, ____ and ∠7
   ∠2 and ____, ____ and ____

b. ∠1 and ____, ____ and ____

c. ____ and ∠8, ____ and ____

d. ____ and ____, ____ and ∠8

✔ *Checkpoint* Complete the statement using *corresponding, alternate exterior, alternate interior,* or *consecutive interior.*

5. ∠9 and ∠11 are _____ angles.

6. ∠6 and ∠10 are _____ angles.

7. ∠8 and ∠11 are _____ angles.

8. ∠7 and ∠13 are _____ angles.

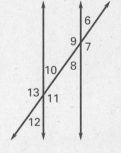

3.2 Proof and Perpendicular Lines

Goals • Write different types of proofs.
• Prove results about perpendicular lines.

VOCABULARY

Flow proof

THEOREM 3.1

If two lines intersect to form a
linear pair of congruent angles,
then the lines are

_____.

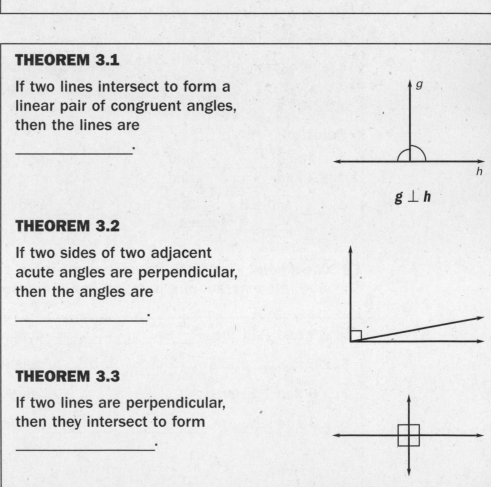

$g \perp h$

THEOREM 3.2

If two sides of two adjacent
acute angles are perpendicular,
then the angles are

_____.

THEOREM 3.3

If two lines are perpendicular,
then they intersect to form

_____.

Example 1 **Comparing Types of Proofs**

Given: $m\angle AEC = m\angle DEB$

Prove: $m\angle AEB = m\angle DEC$

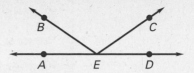

Method 1 Two-column Proof

Statements	Reasons
1. $m\angle AEC = $ _____	1. Given
2. $m\angle AEB + m\angle$ _____ $= m\angle AEC$	2. Angle Addition Postulate
3. $m\angle AEB + m\angle BEC = m\angle$ _____	3. Substitution Property of Equality
4. $m\angle DEC + m\angle BEC = m\angle$ _____	4. Angle Addition Postulate
5. $m\angle$ _____ $+ m\angle$ _____ $= m\angle$ _____ $+ m\angle$ _____	5. Transitive Property of Equality
6. $m\angle AEB = m\angle DEC$	6. _____

Method 2 Paragraph Proof

By the Angle Addition Postulate, $m\angle$ _____ $+ m\angle$ _____ $= m\angle AEC$. Using the Substitution Property of Equality and the given fact that $m\angle AEC = m\angle$ _____ , you can conclude that $m\angle AEB + m\angle$ _____ $= m\angle DEB$. Using the Angle Addition Postulate and the Transitive Property of Equality, you can show that $m\angle$ _____ $+ m\angle$ _____ $= m\angle$ _____ $+ m\angle$ _____ . It follows from the _____ _____ that $m\angle AEB = m\angle DEC$.

Method 3 Flow Proof

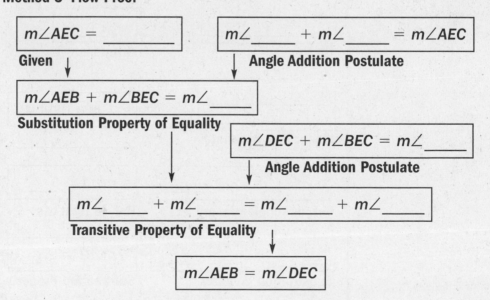

Example 2   *Proof of Theorem 3.2*

Given: $\overrightarrow{BA} \perp \overrightarrow{BC}$

Prove: $\angle 1$ and $\angle 2$ are complementary.

Plan for Proof Use $m\angle ABC = 90°$ and $m\angle 1 + m\angle 2 = m\angle ABC$ to show that $\angle 1$ and $\angle 2$ are complementary.

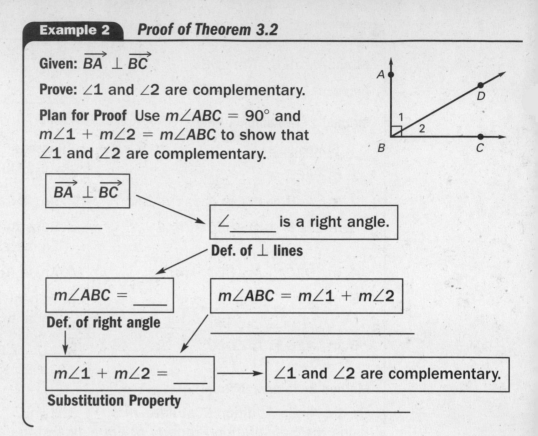

$$\boxed{\overrightarrow{BA} \perp \overrightarrow{BC}}$$
_____

$$\boxed{\angle \underline{\quad} \text{ is a right angle.}}$$
Def. of $\perp$ lines

$$\boxed{m\angle ABC = \underline{\quad}}$$
Def. of right angle

$$\boxed{m\angle ABC = m\angle 1 + m\angle 2}$$
_____

$$\boxed{m\angle 1 + m\angle 2 = \underline{\quad}}$$
Substitution Property

$$\boxed{\angle 1 \text{ and } \angle 2 \text{ are complementary.}}$$
_____

✔ **Checkpoint** Complete the flow proof of Theorem 3.3.

1. Given: $j \perp k$, $\angle 1$ and $\angle 2$ are a linear pair.
   Prove: $\angle 2$ is a right angle.

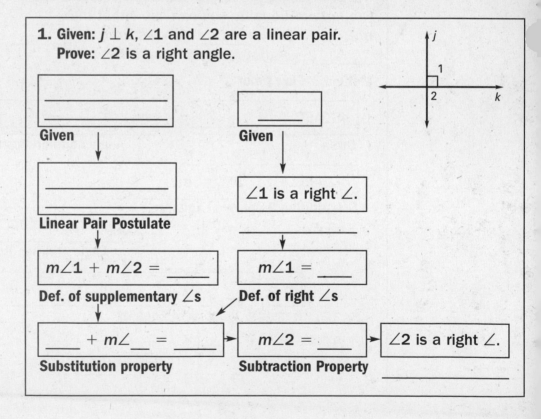

$$\boxed{}$$
Given

$$\boxed{}$$
Given

$$\boxed{}$$
Linear Pair Postulate

$$\boxed{\angle 1 \text{ is a right } \angle.}$$
_____

$$\boxed{m\angle 1 + m\angle 2 = \underline{\quad}}$$
Def. of supplementary $\angle$s

$$\boxed{m\angle 1 = \underline{\quad}}$$
Def. of right $\angle$s

$$\boxed{\underline{\quad} + m\angle\underline{\quad} = \underline{\quad}}$$
Substitution property

$$\boxed{m\angle 2 = \underline{\quad}}$$
Subtraction Property

$$\boxed{\angle 2 \text{ is a right } \angle.}$$
_____

3.3 Parallel Lines and Transversals

Goals • Prove and use results about parallel lines and transversals.
• Use properties of parallel lines to solve problems.

POSTULATE 15: CORRESPONDING ANGLES POSTULATE

If two parallel lines are cut by a transversal,
then the pairs of corresponding angles
are _____.

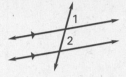

$\angle 1 \cong \angle 2$

THEOREM 3.4: ALTERNATE INTERIOR ANGLES

If two parallel lines are cut by a transversal,
then the pairs of alternate interior angles
are _____.

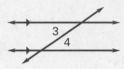

$\angle 3 \cong \angle 4$

THEOREM 3.5: CONSECUTIVE INTERIOR ANGLES

If two parallel lines are cut by a transversal,
then the pairs of consecutive interior angles
are _____.

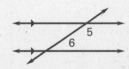

$m\angle 5 + m\angle 6 = 180°$

THEOREM 3.6: ALTERNATE EXTERIOR ANGLES

If two parallel lines are cut by a transversal,
then the pairs of alternate exterior angles
are _____.

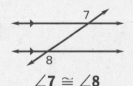

$\angle 7 \cong \angle 8$

THEOREM 3.7: PERPENDICULAR TRANSVERSAL

If a transversal is perpendicular to one of two
parallel lines, then it is _____ to
the other.

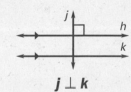

$j \perp k$

Example 1   *Using Properties of Parallel Lines*

Given that $m\angle 1 = 118°$, find each measure. Tell which postulate or theorem you use.

a. $\angle 2$ b. $\angle 3$ c. $\angle 5$ d. $\angle 4$

Solution

a. $m\angle 2 = 180° - m\angle \underline{} = \underline{}°$ _____

b. $m\angle 3 = m\angle \underline{} = \underline{}°$ _____
    _____

c. $m\angle 5 = m\angle \underline{} = \underline{}°$ _____
    _____

d. $m\angle 4 = m\angle \underline{} = \underline{}°$ _____
    _____

Example 2   *Using Properties of Parallel Lines*

Parking Lot Design In the diagram of the parking lot, $m \parallel n$. What is $m\angle 1$?

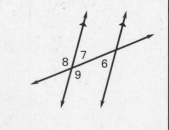

Solution

$m\angle 1 + 80° = \underline{}°$ _____
    _____

$m\angle 1 = \underline{}°$ _____ **Property of Equality**

✔ *Checkpoint* Given that $m\angle 6 = 53°$, find the angle measure. Tell which postulate or theorem you use.

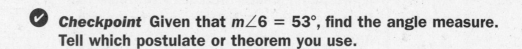

1. $\angle 7$

2. $\angle 8$

3. $\angle 9$

Example 3   *Using Properties of Parallel Lines*

Use properties of parallel lines to find the
value of *x*.

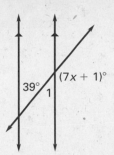

Solution

$$m\angle 1 = \underline{}°$$ _____

_____

$$m\angle 1 + (7x + 1)° = \underline{}°$$ _____

$$\underline{}° + (7x + 1)° = \underline{}°$$ **Substitute.**

$$7x = \underline{}$$ **Subtract.**

$$x = \underline{}$$ **Divide.**

✓ *Checkpoint* Use properties of parallel lines to find the value
of *x*.

4.	5.
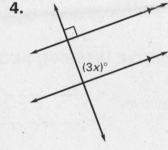	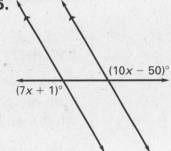

3.4 Proving Lines are Parallel

Goals • Prove that two lines are parallel.
• Use properties of parallel lines to solve problems.

POSTULATE 16: CORRESPONDING ANGLES CONVERSE

If two lines are cut by a transversal so that corresponding angles are _____, then the lines are parallel.

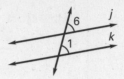

If ∠1 ≅ ∠6, then *j* ∥ *k*.

THEOREM 3.8: ALTERNATE INTERIOR ANGLES CONVERSE

If two lines are cut by a transversal so that alternate interior angles are _____, then the lines are parallel.

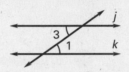

If ∠1 ≅ ∠3, then *j* ∥ *k*.

THEOREM 3.9: CONSECUTIVE INTERIOR ANGLES CONVERSE

If two lines are cut by a transversal so that consecutive interior angles are _____, then the lines are parallel.

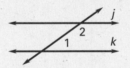

If *m*∠1 + *m*∠2 = 180°, then *j* ∥ *k*.

THEOREM 3.10: ALTERNATE EXTERIOR ANGLES CONVERSE

If two lines are cut by a transversal so that alternate exterior angles are _____, then the lines are parallel.

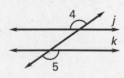

If ∠4 ≅ ∠5, then *j* ∥ *k*.

Example 1 **Proof of the Alternate Exterior Angles Converse**

Prove the Alternate
Exterior Angles Converse.

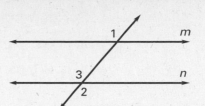

Solution

Given: $\angle 1 \cong \angle 2$

Prove: $m \parallel n$

Statements	Reasons
1. $\angle 1 \cong \angle 2$	1. _____
2. $\angle 2 \cong \angle 3$	2. _____
3. $\angle\_\_ \cong \angle\_\_$	3. Transitive Property of Congruence
4. $m \parallel n$	4. _____

Example 2 **Applying the Alternate Interior Angles Converse**

Find the value of x that
makes $p \parallel q$.

Lines p and q will be parallel
if the marked angles are

_____.

$$\underline{\quad} + \underline{\quad} = \underline{\quad} - \underline{\quad}$$
$$\underline{\quad} x + \underline{\quad} = \underline{\quad} x$$
$$\underline{\quad} = \underline{\quad} x$$
$$\underline{\quad} = x$$

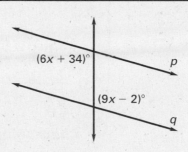

✔ **Checkpoint** Find the value of x that makes $p \parallel q$.

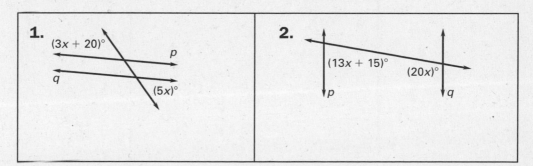

1.

2.

Example 3   *Identifying Parallel Lines*

Decide which lines are parallel.

a. Is $\overleftrightarrow{AG}$ parallel to $\overleftrightarrow{CE}$?

b. Is $\overleftrightarrow{BH}$ parallel to $\overleftrightarrow{DF}$?

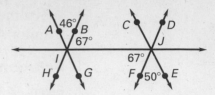

Solution

a. Decide whether $\overleftrightarrow{AG}$ is parallel to $\overleftrightarrow{CE}$.

$m\angle AIJ = $ _____ + _____ = _____

$m\angle EJI = $ _____ + _____ = _____

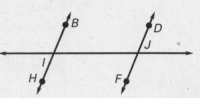

Answer $\angle AIJ$ and $\angle EJI$ are _____ angles that are _____ . So, $\overleftrightarrow{AG}$ and $\overleftrightarrow{CE}$ are _____ .

b. Decide whether $\overleftrightarrow{BH}$ is parallel to $\overleftrightarrow{DF}$.

$m\angle BIJ = $ _____

$m\angle FJI = $ _____

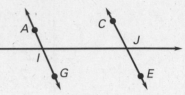

Answer $\angle BIJ$ and $\angle FJI$ are _____ angles that are _____ . So, $\overleftrightarrow{BH}$ and $\overleftrightarrow{DF}$ are _____ .

✓ **Checkpoint** Decide whether $\overrightarrow{BA}$ is parallel to $\overrightarrow{DE}$. Explain.

3.

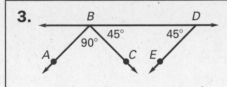

4.

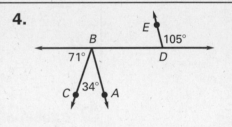

3.5 Using Properties of Parallel Lines

Goals • Use properties of parallel lines in real-life situations.
• Construct parallel lines using a straightedge and a compass.

THEOREM 3.11

If two lines are parallel to the same line, then they are _____ to each other.

If $p \parallel q$ and $q \parallel r$, then $p \parallel r$.

THEOREM 3.12

In a plane, if two lines are perpendicular to the same line, then they are _____ to each other.

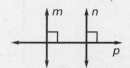

If $m \perp p$ and $n \perp p$, then $m \parallel n$.

Example 1   *Explaining Why Fence Posts are Parallel*

In the diagram at the right, each fence post is parallel to the fence post immediately to the right. Explain why the fence posts on each end are parallel.

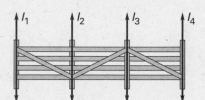

Solution

You are given that $l_1 \parallel$ ___ and $l_2 \parallel$ ___ . By Theorem 3.11, ___ $\parallel$ ___ .

You are also given that $l_3 \parallel$ ___ . Because ___ $\parallel$ ___ and ___ $\parallel$ ___ , you

can use Theorem 3.11 again to conclude that $l_1 \parallel l_4$.

Example 2 **Building a Picture Frame**

You are building the picture frame in the diagram at the right. You cut pieces of wood such that the measures of ∠1 and ∠4 are 30° and the measures of ∠2 and ∠3 are 60°. Prove that the right and left sides of the frame are parallel.

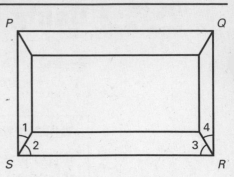

Solution

Given: $m\angle 1 = $ ___°; $m\angle 2 = $ ___°; $m\angle 3 = $ ___°; $m\angle 4 = $ ___°

Prove: ____ ∥ ____

Statements	Reasons
1. $m\angle 1 = $ ___°, $m\angle 2 = $ ___° $m\angle 3 = $ ___°, $m\angle 4 = $ ___°	1. _____
2. $m\angle PSR = m\angle$ ___ $+ m\angle$ ___ $m\angle QRS = m\angle$ ___ $+ m\angle$ ___	2. Angle Addition Postulate
3. $m\angle PSR = $ ___° $m\angle QRS = $ ___°	3. Substitution property
4. ∠PSR is a _____. ∠QRS is a _____.	4. _____
5. $\overline{PS} \perp \overline{SR}$ $\overline{QR} \perp \overline{RS}$	5. _____
6. ____ ∥ ____	6. _____ _____ .

✔ *Checkpoint* **Complete the following exercise.**

1. Are all the vertical lines parallel? Explain.

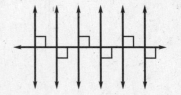

ACTIVITY: CONSTRUCTING PARALLEL LINES

Use the following steps to draw a line that passes through a given point P and is parallel to a given line m.

1. Draw points Q and R on line m.

2. Draw $\overleftrightarrow{PQ}$.

3. Draw an arc with the compass point at Q so that it crosses $\overleftrightarrow{PQ}$ and $\overleftrightarrow{QR}$.

4. Using the same radius, draw an arc with center P. Label the intersection of the arc and $\overleftrightarrow{PQ}$ as T.

5. Using the point where the initial arc intersects $\overleftrightarrow{PQ}$ as the center, draw an arc that passes through the intersection of the initial arc and $\overleftrightarrow{QR}$.

6. Using the same radius, draw an arc with center T that intersects the arc through T. Label the intersection as S. (Point S must be in the interior of ∠PQR.)

7. Draw $\overleftrightarrow{PS}$.

P
●

m

3.6 Parallel Lines in the Coordinate Plane

Goals
- Find slopes of lines and use slope to identify parallel lines in a coordinate plane.
- Write equations of parallel lines in a coordinate plane.

Example 1 *Finding the Slope of a Line*

Find the slope of the line that passes through the points $(-4, -3)$ and $(5, 3)$.

Solution

Let $(x_1, y_1) = (\underline{\quad}, \underline{\quad})$ and $(x_2, y_2) = (\underline{\quad}, \underline{\quad})$.

$$m = \frac{y_2 - y_1}{x_2 - x_1}$$

$$= \frac{\boxed{} - \left(\boxed{}\right)}{\boxed{} - \left(\boxed{}\right)}$$

$$= \underline{\quad} = \underline{\quad}$$

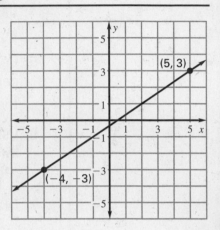

Answer The slope of the line is $\underline{\quad}$.

POSTULATE 17: SLOPES OF PARALLEL LINES

In a coordinate plane, two nonvertical lines are parallel if and only if they have the same _____. Any two vertical lines are parallel.

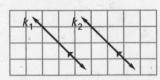

Lines k_1 and k_2 have the same _____.

Example 2   *Identifying Parallel Lines*

Find the slope of each line. Which lines are parallel?

Solution

Find the slope of j_1. Line j_1 passes through (___ , __) and (___ , ___).

$$m_1 = \frac{\boxed{} - \boxed{}}{\boxed{} - \left(\boxed{}\right)} = \frac{}{\rule{1cm}{0.4pt}} = \rule{0.8cm}{0.4pt}$$

Find the slope of j_2. Line j_2 passes through (___ , __) and (__ , __).

$$m_2 = \frac{\boxed{} - \boxed{}}{\boxed{} - \left(\boxed{}\right)} = \frac{}{\rule{1cm}{0.4pt}} = \rule{0.8cm}{0.4pt}$$

Find the slope of j_3. Line j_3 passes through (__ , __) and (__ , __).

$$m_3 = \frac{\boxed{} - \boxed{}}{\boxed{} - \boxed{}} = \rule{1.5cm}{0.4pt}$$

Answer Compare the slopes. Lines ___ and ___ are parallel.

✔ *Checkpoint* Complete the following exercises.

1. Find the slope of the line that passes through the points $(-2, 5)$ and $(3, 0)$.	**2.** Find the slope of each line. Are the lines parallel? 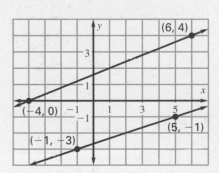

Example 3 *Writing an Equation of a Parallel Line*

Line k_1 has the equation $y = -2x + 5$.

Line k_2 is parallel to k_1 and passes through the point $(-4, 3)$. Write an equation of k_2.

Solution

Find the slope of each line.

The slope of k_1 is ____. Because parallel lines have the same _____, the slope of k_2 is ____.

Find the y-intercept. Use $(x, y) = ($ ____ , __ $)$ and $m = $ ____ .

$y = mx + b$	Write _____ form.
__ = ____(____ $) + b$	Substitute values.
__ = __ $+ b$	Multiply.
____ $= b$	Subtract ___ from each side.

Answer Because $m = $ ____ and $b = $ ____ , an equation of k_2 is $y = $ _____ .

✔ *Checkpoint* Write an equation of the line that passes through point P and is parallel to the line with the given equation.

3. $P(0, -3)$, $y = x + 7$	**4.** $P(2, 3)$, $y = -\dfrac{3}{2}x - 1$

3.7 Perpendicular Lines in the Coordinate Plane

Goals • Use slope to identify perpendicular lines in coordinate planes.
• Write equations of perpendicular lines.

POSTULATE 18: SLOPES OF PERPENDICULAR LINES

In a coordinate plane, two nonvertical lines are perpendicular if and only if the product of their slopes is ____.

Vertical and horizontal lines are _____.

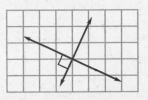

product of slopes $= 2\left(-\dfrac{1}{2}\right) =$ ____

Example 1   *Deciding Whether Lines are Perpendicular*

Decide whether $j_1 \perp j_2$.

Solution
Find the slope of each line.

Slope of $j_1 = \dfrac{\boxed{} - \boxed{}}{\boxed{} - \boxed{}}$

$= \underline{} = \underline{}$

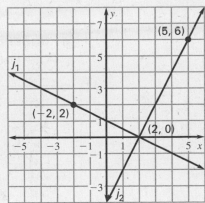

Slope of $j_2 = \dfrac{\boxed{} - \boxed{}}{\boxed{} - \boxed{}} = \underline{} = \underline{}$

Multiply the slopes.

Answer The product is $\left(\underline{}\right)\left(\underline{}\right) =$ ____, so _____.

Example 2 **Deciding Whether Lines are Perpendicular**

Decide whether the lines are perpendicular.

line *s*: $3x - 2y = 1$ line *t*: $6x + 9y = 3$

Solution

Rewrite each equation in slope-intercept form to find the slope.

line *s*: $3x - 2y = 1$ line *t*: $6x + 9y = 3$

$$-2y = \underline{\hspace{1cm}} + 1$$ $$9y = \underline{\hspace{1cm}} + 3$$

$$y = \underline{\hspace{2cm}}$$ $$y = \underline{\hspace{2cm}}$$

> The slope-intercept form of a linear equation is $y = mx + b$ where *m* is the slope and *b* is the *y*-intercept.

slope = $\underline{\hspace{1cm}}$ $y = \underline{\hspace{2cm}}$

slope = $\underline{\hspace{1cm}}$

Multiply the slopes to see if the lines are perpendicular.

The product of the slopes is $\underline{\hspace{1cm}}$.

Answer So, lines *s* and *t* are $\underline{\hspace{3cm}}$.

✔ **Checkpoint** Find the slopes of the lines. Then decide whether the lines are perpendicular.

1.

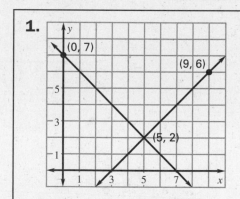

2. line k_1: $6x + 2y = 8$

line k_2: $y = -3x - 4$

Example 3   *Writing the Equation of a Perpendicular Line*

Line r_1 has equation $y = 3x + 5$. Find an equation of the line r_2 that passes through $P(3, 1)$ and is perpendicular to r_1.

Solution

Find the slope of r_2. Let m_1 and m_2 represent the slopes of r_1 and r_2.

$m_1 \cdot m_2 = $ _____   **The product of the slopes of $\perp$ lines is** _____ .

_____ $\cdot m_2 = $ _____   **Substitute for m_1.**

$m_2 = \dfrac{}{}$ **Solve for m_2.**

Then use $m_2 = \dfrac{}{}$ and $(x, y) = ($ __ , __ $)$ to find b.

$y = m_2 x + b$ **Slope-intercept form**

__ $= \dfrac{}{} ($ __ $) + b$ **Substitute for y, m_2, and x.**

__ $= b$ **Simplify.**

Answer So, an equation of r_2 is $y = $ _____ .

✔ *Checkpoint* **Find an equation of the line that passes through the given point and is perpendicular to the given line.**

3. $(0, -4)$, $y = -x$	**4.** $(2, -2)$, $y = \dfrac{1}{4}x + 10$

Words to Review

Give an example of the vocabulary word.

Parallel lines	Skew lines
Parallel planes	Transversal
Corresponding angles	Alternate interior angles

Alternate exterior angles	Consecutive interior angles
Same side interior angles	Flow proof

Review your notes and Chapter 3 by using the Chapter Review on pages 180–182 of your textbook.

4.1 Triangles and Angles

Goals • Classify triangles by their sides and angles.
       • Find angle measures in triangles.

VOCABULARY

Triangle

Vertex

Adjacent sides

Legs

Hypotenuse

Base

Interior angles

Exterior angles

Corollary

NAMES OF TRIANGLES

Classification by Sides

_____   _____   _____
_____   _____   _____

3 congruent sides   At least 2 congruent   No congruent sides
                     sides

Classification by Angles

_____ _____ _____ _____
_____ _____ _____ _____

3 acute angles   3 congruent   1 right angle   1 obtuse angle
                  angles

Example 1   *Classifying Triangles*

Classify each triangle. Be as specific as possible.

a. △ABC has two acute angles, one right angle and two congruent sides. It is a

_____.

b. △DEF has one obtuse angle and no congruent sides. It is an _____.

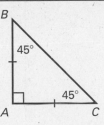

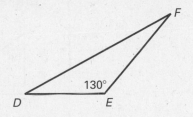

THEOREM 4.1: TRIANGLE SUM THEOREM

The sum of the measures of the interior angles of a triangle is _____.

$m\angle A + m\angle B + m\angle C =$ _____

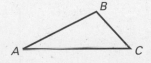

THEOREM 4.2: EXTERIOR ANGLE THEOREM

The measure of an exterior angle of a
triangle is equal to the sum of the measures
of the two nonadjacent interior angles.

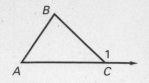

$m\angle 1 =$ _____ + _____

COROLLARY TO THE TRIANGLE SUM THEOREM

The acute angles of a right triangle are
complementary.

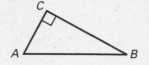

$m\angle A + m\angle B =$ _____

Example 2   *Finding an Angle Measure*

You can apply the Exterior Angle Theorem to
find the measure of the exterior angle shown.
First write and solve an equation to find the
value of x:

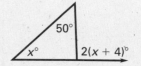

$x° + 50° = 2(x + 4)°$ **Apply the Exterior Angle Theorem.**

_____ $= x$ **Solve for x.**

Answer So, the measure of the exterior angle is $2 \cdot ($ _____ $+ 4)°$,
or _____ °.

✔ *Checkpoint* Complete the following exercises.

1. Classify the triangle by its
angles and by its sides.

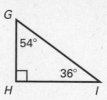

2. Find the measure of the
exterior angle shown.

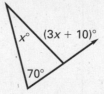

4.2 Congruence and Triangles

Goals • Identify congruent figures and corresponding parts.
• Prove that two triangles are congruent.

VOCABULARY

Congruent

Corresponding angles

Corresponding sides

Example 1 *Naming Congruent Parts*

Write a congruence statement for the triangles. Identify all pairs of congruent corresponding parts.

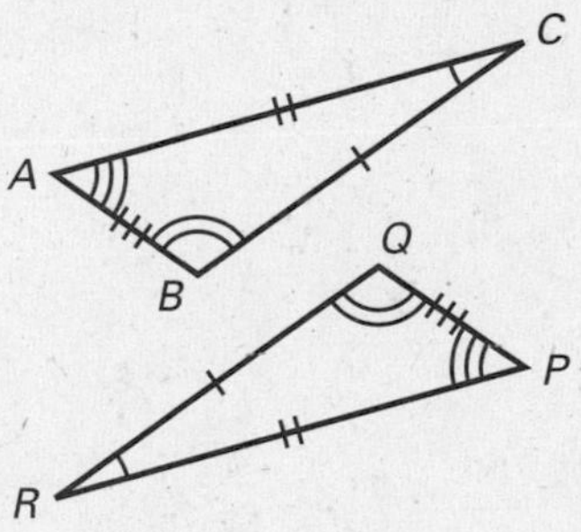

Solution

The diagram indicates that △_____ ≅ △_____.

The congruent angles and sides are as follows.

Angles: _____, _____, _____

Sides: _____, _____, _____

Example 2 **Using Properties of Congruent Figures**

In the diagram, $DEFG \cong KLMN$.

a. Find the value of x.

b. Find the value of y.

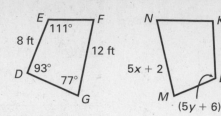

Solution

a. You know that $\overline{FG} \cong \overline{MN}$.

So, $FG = MN$.

$12 = 5x + 2$ Substitute for ____ and ____.

____ $= 5x$ Subtract __ from each side.

____ $= x$ Divide each side by __.

b. You know that $\angle E \cong \angle L$.

So, $m\angle E = m\angle L$.

$111° = (5y + 6)°$ Substitute for _____ and _____.

____ $= 5y$ Subtract __ from each side.

____ $= y$ Divide each side by __.

THEOREM 4.3: THIRD ANGLES THEOREM

If two angles of one triangle are congruent to two angles of another triangle, then the third angles are also congruent.

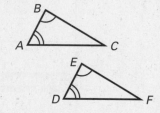

If $\angle A \cong \angle D$ and $\angle B \cong \angle E$, then _____.

Example 3   *Using the Third Angles Theorem*

Find the value of *x*.

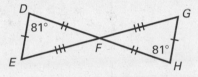

Solution

In the diagram, $\angle V \cong \angle Y$ and $\angle U \cong \angle Z$. From the Third Angles Theorem, you know that $\angle W \cong \angle X$. So, $m\angle W = m\angle X$. From the Triangle Sum Theorem, $m\angle W = 180° - 54° - 67° = $ ___°.

$m\angle W = m\angle X$	**Third Angles Theorem**
___° $= (4x - 5)°$	**Substitute.**
___ $= 4x$	**Add ___ to each side.**
___ $= x$	**Divide each side by ___.**

Example 4   *Determining Whether Triangles are Congruent*

Decide whether the triangles are congruent. Justify your reasoning.

Solution

Paragraph Proof From the diagram, you are given that all three pairs of corresponding sides are congruent.

$\overline{DE} \cong$ ____, ____ $\cong \overline{GF}$, $\overline{DF} \cong$ ____

Because $\angle D$ and $\angle H$ have the same measure, $\angle D \cong \angle H$. By the Vertical Angles Theorem, you know that _____.

By the Third Angles Theorem, _____.

Answer So, all three pairs of corresponding sides and all three pairs of corresponding angles are _____. By the definition of congruent triangles, _____.

THEOREM 4.4: PROPERTIES OF CONGRUENT TRIANGLES

Reflexive Property of Congruent Triangles

Every triangle is congruent to _____ .

Symmetric Property of Congruent Triangles

If △ABC ≅ △DEF, then _____ .

Transitive Property of Congruent Triangles

If △ABC ≅ △DEF and △DEF ≅ △JKL, then

_____ .

✔ *Checkpoint* Complete the following exercises.

1. Find the value of *x*.

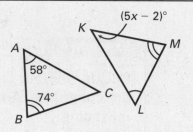

2. Decide whether the triangles are congruent. Justify your reasoning.

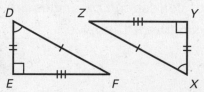

4.3 Proving Triangles are Congruent: SSS and SAS

Goals • Prove that triangles are congruent using the SSS and SAS Congruence Postulates.
• Use congruence postulates in real-life problems.

POSTULATE 19: SIDE-SIDE-SIDE (SSS) CONGRUENCE POSTULATE

If three sides of one triangle are congruent to three sides of a second triangle, then the two triangles are congruent.

If   Side $\overline{MN} \cong$ _____,

       Side $\overline{NP} \cong$ _____, and

       Side $\overline{PM} \cong$ _____,

then $\triangle MNP \cong$ _____.

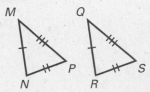

Example 1   *Using the SSS Congruence Postulate*

Prove that $\triangle DEF \cong \triangle JKL$.

Solution

Paragraph Proof The marks on the diagram show that $\overline{DE} \cong$ _____, _____ $\cong \overline{KL}$, and $\overline{DF} \cong$ _____.

Answer So, by the _____, you know that _____ $\cong$ _____.

POSTULATE 20: SIDE-ANGLE-SIDE (SAS) CONGRUENCE POSTULATE

If two sides and the included angle of one triangle are congruent to two sides and the included angle of a second triangle, then the two triangles are congruent.

If   Side $\overline{PQ} \cong$ _____,

       Angle $\angle Q \cong$ _____, and

       Side $\overline{QS} \cong$ _____,

then $\triangle PQS \cong$ _____.

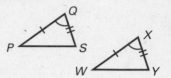

Example 2   *Using the SAS Congruence Postulate*

Prove that $\triangle SYT \cong \triangle WYX$.

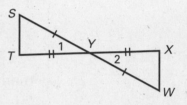

Statements	Reasons
1. $\overline{TY} \cong$ ____, $\overline{SY} \cong$ _____	1. Given
2. $\angle 1 \cong \angle 2$	2. _____
3. $\triangle SYT \cong \triangle WYX$	3. _____

✔ **Checkpoint** Complete the following exercise.

1. Prove that $\triangle FGT \cong \triangle RST$.

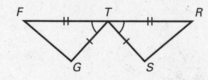

Example 3 _Choosing a Congruence Postulate to Use_

Decide whether enough information is given in the diagram to prove that △WYZ ≅ △ZXW. If there is enough information, state the congruence postulate you would use.

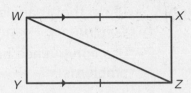

Solution

Paragraph Proof The marks on the diagram show that
_____ ≅ _____ and _____ ‖ _____. By the Alternate Interior Angles Postulate, _____ ≅ _____. By the Reflexive Property of Congruence, _____ ≅ _____. Because two sides and the included angle of △WYZ are congruent to the corresponding two sides and included angle of △ZXW, you can use the _____
_____ to prove that the triangles are congruent.

✔ _Checkpoint_ **Decide whether enough information is given to prove that the triangles are congruent. If there is enough information, state the congruence postulate you would use.**

2. △PTQ ≅ △STR	**3.** △CMG ≅ △ZMG
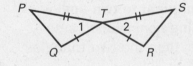	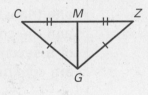

4.4 Proving Triangles are Congruent: ASA and AAS

Goals • Prove that triangles are congruent using the ASA
Congruence Postulate and the AAS Congruence Theorem.
• Use congruence postulates and theorems in real-life
problems.

**POSTULATE 21: ANGLE-SIDE-ANGLE (ASA)
CONGRUENCE POSTULATE**

If two angles and the included side of one
triangle are congruent to two angles and
the included side of a second triangle,
then the two triangles are congruent.

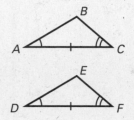

If   Angle $\angle A \cong$ _____,

    Side $\overline{AC} \cong$ _____, and

    Angle $\angle C \cong$ _____,

then $\triangle ABC \cong$ _____.

**THEOREM 4.5: ANGLE-ANGLE-SIDE (AAS)
CONGRUENCE THEOREM**

If two angles and a nonincluded side of
one triangle are congruent to two angles
and the corresponding nonincluded side
of a second triangle, then the two triangles
are congruent.

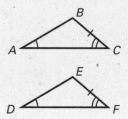

If   Angle $\angle A \cong$ _____,

    Angle $\angle C \cong$ _____, and

    Side   _____ $\cong$ _____,

then $\triangle ABC \cong$ _____.

Example 1 *Developing Proof*

Is it possible to prove that the triangles are congruent? If so, state the postulate or theorem you would use. Explain your reasoning.

a.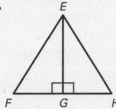

b.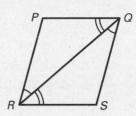

Solution

a. The diagram shows that ∠EGH and ∠EGF are right angles. So, ∠_____ ≅ ∠_____ . Also, _____ ≅ _____ by the Reflexive Property of Congruence. This is _____ information to prove that the triangles are congruent.

b. In addition to the angles that are marked, _____ ≅ _____ by the Reflexive Property of Congruence. _____ of corresponding angles and the one pair of corresponding _____ are congruent. You can use the _____ to prove that _____ ≅ _____ .

Example 2 *Proving Triangles are Congruent*

Given: $\overline{WY} \parallel \overline{XZ}$, ∠Y ≅ ∠X

Prove: △WYZ ≅ △ZXW

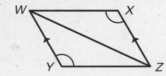

Plan for Proof You are given that ∠Y ≅ ∠X. Use the fact that $\overline{WY} \parallel \overline{XZ}$ to identify a pair of congruent angles.

Statements	Reasons
1. _____ ≅ _____ , _____ ∥ _____	1. Given
2. _____ ≅ _____	2. Alternate Interior Angles Theorem
3. _____ ≅ _____	3. Reflexive Property of Congruence
4. _____ ≅ _____	4. _____

Example 3   *Using Properties of Congruent Triangles*

Cliff Diving At a cliff-diving competition, you and a friend stand at different locations (points *F* and *Y*) along the shore. To record the spot where a diver enters the water, you find the angle between each of your sightlines and $\overline{FY}$. Assuming your sightlines are accurate, do you have enough information to record a diver's entry data?

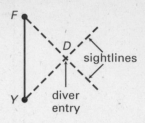

Solution

Think of points *F* and *Y* as two vertices of a triangle. The diver's entry spot *D* is the other vertex. You know $m\angle F$ and $m\angle Y$. You also know the length of the included side $\overline{FY}$. From the _____ , you can conclude that any two triangles with these measurements are _____ . In other words, there is only one triangle with the given measurements and location.

Answer _____

_____

✔ *Checkpoint* **Complete the following exercises.**

1. Given: *R* is the midpoint of $\overline{QS}$; $\angle QRP \cong \angle SRT$; $\angle Q$ and $\angle S$ are right angles. **Prove:** $\triangle QRP \cong \triangle SRT$ 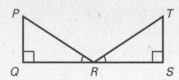	**2.** A kite falls into a field E 35° N from where you stand. Your friend, standing 75 yards from you, did not see the kite fall. Is there enough information to locate the kite after it fell?

Using Congruent Triangles

Goals • Use congruent triangles to plan and write proofs.
• Use congruent triangles to prove constructions are valid.

Example 1 *Planning and Writing a Proof*

Given: $\overline{SD} \cong \overline{TC}$, $\overline{CS} \cong \overline{DT}$

Prove: $\angle SCT \cong \angle TDS$

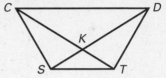

Plan for Proof Show that $\triangle TDS \cong \triangle SCT$. Then use the fact that corresponding parts of congruent triangles are congruent.

Solution

Mark the diagram at the right with the given information. Then mark any additional information that you can deduce. Because $\overline{ST}$ is the same segment in both triangles, you can deduce that $\overline{ST} \cong \overline{ST}$.

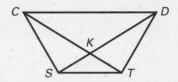

Paragraph Proof By the Reflexive Property of Congruence, _____ $\cong$ _____ . You can use the _____ Congruence Postulate to conclude that _____ $\cong$ _____ . Finally, because corresponding parts of congruent triangles are congruent, it follows that _____ $\cong$ _____ .

✔ **Checkpoint** Complete the following exercise.

1. Given: $\angle WYX \cong \angle ZXY$, $\angle WXY \cong \angle ZYX$
   Prove: $\overline{WX} \cong \overline{ZY}$

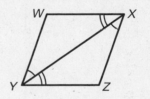

Example 2   *Using More than One Pair of Triangles*

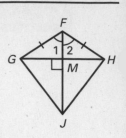

Given: $\angle GMJ$ and $\angle HMJ$ are right angles,
$\overline{GF} \cong \overline{HF}$, $\angle 1 \cong \angle 2$

Prove: $\angle GJM \cong \angle HJM$

Plan for Proof Prove that $\triangle GJM \cong \triangle HJM$. Then use the fact that corresponding parts of congruent triangles are congruent to show that _____ $\cong$ _____.

Statements	Reasons
1. $\overline{GF} \cong \overline{HF}$, $\angle 1 \cong \angle 2$	1. Given
2. ____ $\cong$ ____	2. Reflexive Prop. of Cong.
3. $\triangle FGM \cong \triangle FHM$	3. _____
4. $\overline{GM} \cong \overline{MH}$	4. _____
5. _____ $\cong$ _____	5. Right angles are congruent.
6. $\overline{MJ} \cong \overline{MJ}$	6. _____
7. $\triangle GJM \cong \triangle HJM$	7. _____
8. _____ $\cong$ _____	8. Corres. parts of $\cong$ $\triangle$s are $\cong$.

✔ **Checkpoint** Complete the following exercise.

2. Given: $\angle NZY$, $\angle QZY$, $\angle MXY$, $\angle PXY$ are right angles, $\overline{YN} \cong \overline{YQ}$, $\angle N \cong \angle Q$

Prove: $\triangle MYX \cong \triangle PYX$

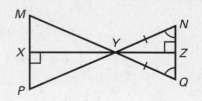

Example 3   *Proving a Construction*

The construction shows ∠*GHJ* bisected by $\overrightarrow{HK}$. Write a proof to verify that the construction is valid.

Plan for Proof Show that △*HGK* ≅ △*HJK*. Then show that ∠1 ≅ ∠2. By construction, you can assume the following statements as given.

$\overline{HG} \cong \overline{HJ}$ Same compass setting is used.

$\overline{GK} \cong \overline{JK}$ Same compass setting is used.

Solution

Statements	Reasons
1. _____ ≅ _____	1. Given
2. _____ ≅ _____	2. Given
3. $\overline{HK} \cong \overline{HK}$	3. _____
4. △*HGK* ≅ △*HJK*	4. _____
5. ∠__ ≅ ∠__	5. Corresp. parts of ≅ △s are ≅.
6. _____	6. Definition of _____

✔ *Checkpoint* Use a straightedge and a compass to perform the construction. Label the important points of your construction. Then write a paragraph proof to verify the results.

3. Bisect a right angle.

4.6 Isosceles, Equilateral, and Right Triangles

Goals • Use properties of isosceles and equilateral triangles.
• Use properties of right triangles.

VOCABULARY

Base angles

Vertex angle

THEOREM 4.6: BASE ANGLES THEOREM

If two sides of a triangle are congruent,
then the angles opposite them are congruent.

If $\overline{AB} \cong \overline{AC}$, then $\angle B \cong \angle$__.

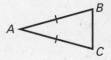

THEOREM 4.7: CONVERSE OF THE BASE ANGLES THEOREM

If two angles of a triangle are congruent,
then the sides opposite them are congruent.

If $\angle B \cong \angle C$, then $\overline{AB} \cong$ ____.

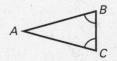

COROLLARY TO THEOREM 4.6

If a triangle is equilateral, then it is equiangular.

COROLLARY TO THEOREM 4.7

If a triangle is equiangular, then it is equilateral.

Example 1 Using Isosceles Triangles

Find the value of y.

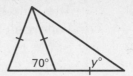

Solution

Notice that y represents the measure of a base angle of an isosceles triangle. From the _____ Theorem, the other base angle has the same measure. The vertex angle forms a linear pair with a 70° angle, so its measure is ____°.

$$110° + \underline{\quad} = 180° \qquad \text{Apply the Triangle Sum Theorem.}$$

$$y = \underline{\quad} \qquad \text{Solve for } y.$$

✔ **Checkpoint** Solve for x and y.

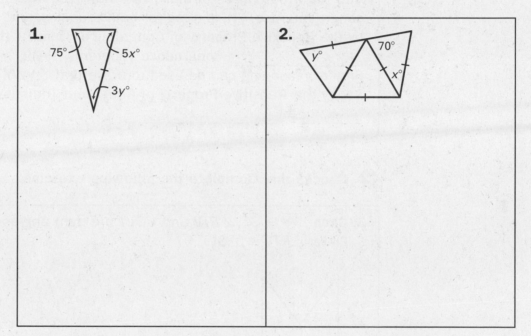

1.

2.

THEOREM 4.8: HYPOTENUSE-LEG (HL) CONGRUENCE THEOREM

If the hypotenuse and a leg of a right triangle are congruent to the hypotenuse and a leg of a second right triangle, then the two triangles are congruent.

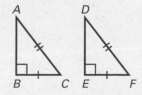

If $\overline{BC} \cong$ ____ and $\overline{AC} \cong$ ____, then $\triangle ABC \cong \triangle$ ____.

Example 2 Proving Right Triangles Congruent

The pole holding up one end of a volleyball net is perpendicular to the plane containing the points *W*, *X*, *Y*, and *Z*. Each of the lines running from the top of the pole to *X*, *Y*, and *Z* uses the same length of rope. Prove that △*VWX*, △*VWY*, and △*VWZ* are congruent.

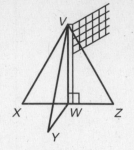

Given: $\overline{VW} \perp \overline{WX}$, $\overline{VW} \perp \overline{WY}$, $\overline{VW} \perp \overline{WZ}$, $\overline{VX} \cong \overline{VY} \cong \overline{VZ}$

Prove: △*VWX* ≅ △*VWY* ≅ △*VWZ*

Paragraph Proof You are given that $\overline{VW} \perp \overline{WX}$ and $\overline{VW} \perp \overline{WY}$, which implies that _____ and _____ are right angles. By definition, _____ and _____ are right triangles. You are given that the hypotenuses of these two triangles, $\overline{VX}$ and $\overline{VY}$, are congruent. Also, $\overline{VW}$ is a leg for both triangles, and _____ ≅ _____ by the Reflexive Property of Congruence. Thus, by the _____ Congruence Theorem, △*VWX* ≅ _____. Similar reasoning can be used to prove that △*VWY* ≅ _____. So, by the Transitive Property of Congruent Triangles, _____ ≅ _____ ≅ _____.

✔ *Checkpoint* **Complete the following exercise.**

3. **Given:** $\overline{RV} \cong \overline{ST}$; ∠*RTV* and ∠*SVT* are right angles
   Prove: △*RTV* ≅ △*SVT*

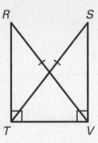

Triangles and Coordinate Proof

Goals • Place geometric figures in a coordinate plane.
• Write a coordinate proof.

VOCABULARY

Coordinate proof

Example 1 *Using the Distance Formula*

A right triangle has legs of 9 units and 12 units. Place the triangle in a coordinate plane. Label the coordinates of the vertices and find the length of the hypotenuse.

Solution

One possible placement is shown. Notice that one leg is vertical and the other leg is horizontal, which assures that the legs meet at right angles. Points on the same vertical segment have the same _____, and the points on the same horizontal segment have the same _____.

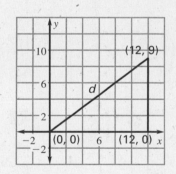

You can use the _____ to find the length of the hypotenuse.

$$d = \sqrt{(x_2 - x_1)^2 + (y_2 - y_1)^2}$$ **Distance Formula**

$$= \sqrt{(\underline{} - \underline{})^2 + (\underline{} - \underline{})^2}$$ **Substitute.**

$$= \sqrt{\underline{}}$$ **Simplify.**

$$= \underline{}$$ **Evaluate square root.**

✔ *Checkpoint* Compete the following exercise.

1. A right triangle has legs of 7.5 units and 4 units. Place the triangle in a coordinate plane. Label the vertices and find the length of the hypotenuse.

Example 2   *Using the Midpoint Formula*

In the diagram, $\triangle WXZ \cong \triangle YXZ$. Find the coordinates of point Z.

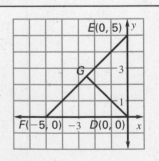

Solution

Because the triangles are congruent, it follows that $\overline{WZ} \cong$ _____. So point Z must be the midpoint of _____. This means you can use the _____ to find the coordinates of point Z.

$$Z(x, y) = \left(\frac{x_1 + x_2}{2}, \frac{y_1 + y_2}{2}\right)$$ **Midpoint Formula**

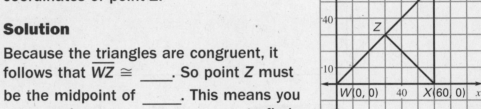

$$= \left(\frac{\square + \square}{2}, \frac{\square + \square}{2}\right)$$ **Substitute.**

$$= (\underline{\quad}, \underline{\quad})$$ **Simplify.**

✔ *Checkpoint* Complete the following exercise.

2. In the diagram, $\triangle DEG \cong \triangle DFG$. Find the coordinates of G.

Example 3 **Writing a Coordinate Proof**

Given: Coordinates of figure *FGJH*
Prove: △*FGH* ≅ △*JHG*

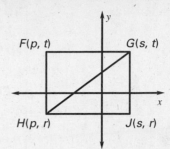

Solution

Use the Distance Formula to find *FG* and *HJ*.

$$FG = \sqrt{(s - p)^2 + (t - t)^2} = \sqrt{(s - p)^2}$$

$$HJ = \sqrt{(s - p)^2 + (r - r)^2} = \sqrt{(s - p)^2}$$

Use the Distance Formula to find *FH* and *GJ*.

$$FH = \sqrt{(p - p)^2 + (r - t)^2} = \sqrt{(r - t)^2}$$

$$GJ = \sqrt{(s - s)^2 + (r - t)^2} = \sqrt{(r - t)^2}$$

So, you can conclude that _____ and _____ . Because $\overline{GH} \cong \overline{GH}$, you can apply the _____ Congruence Postulate to conclude that △*FGH* ≅ △*JHG*.

✔ *Checkpoint* **Complete the following exercise.**

3. Given: Coordinates of figure *ABCD*
   Prove: △*ABC* ≅ △*ADC*

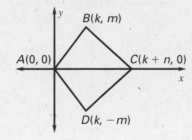

Words to Review

Give an example of the vocabulary word.

Equilateral triangle	Isosceles triangle
Scalene triangle	Acute triangle
Equiangular triangle	Right triangle
Obtuse triangle	Vertex of a triangle
Adjacent sides of a triangle	Legs of a right triangle

Hypotenuse	Legs and base of an isosceles triangle
Interior angle	Exterior angle
Corollary	Congruent
Corresponding angles	Corresponding sides
Base angle and vertex angle	Coordinate proof

Review your notes and Chapter 4 by using the Chapter Review on pages 252–254 of your textbook.

5.1 Perpendiculars and Bisectors

Goals • Use properties of perpendicular bisectors.
• Use properties of angle bisectors to identify equal distances.

VOCABULARY

Perpendicular bisector

Equidistant from two points

Distance from a point to a line

Equidistant from two lines

THEOREM 5.1: PERPENDICULAR BISECTOR THEOREM

If a point is on the perpendicular bisector
of a segment, then it is equidistant from
the _____ of the segment.

If $\overleftrightarrow{CP}$ is the perpendicular bisector of $\overline{AB}$,
then _____ = _____.

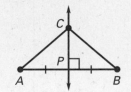

**THEOREM 5.2: CONVERSE OF THE PERPENDICULAR
BISECTOR THEOREM**

If a point is _____ from the endpoints
of a segment, then it is on the perpendicular
bisector of the segment.

If _____ = _____, then *D* lies on the perpendicular
bisector of $\overline{AB}$.

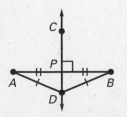

Example 1   *Using Perpendicular Bisectors*

In the diagram shown, $\overrightarrow{BE}$ is the perpendicular bisector of $\overline{AC}$.

a. What segment lengths are equal?

b. $\overline{AP} \cong \overline{CP}$. What can you conclude about point P?

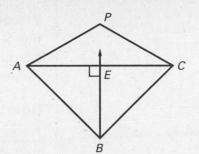

Solution

a. Because $\overrightarrow{BE}$ bisects $\overline{AC}$, ____ = ____.

Because B is on the perpendicular bisector of $\overline{AC}$, you can use the _____ Theorem to conclude that ____ = ____.

b. Because $\overline{AP} \cong \overline{CP}$, $AP =$ ____. Using the _____ _____ Theorem, you can conclude that _____.

THEOREM 5.3: ANGLE BISECTOR THEOREM

If a point is on the bisector of an angle, then it is equidIstant from the two _____ of the angle.

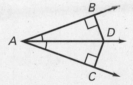

If $m\angle$_____ $= m\angle$_____, then $DB = DC$.

THEOREM 5.4: CONVERSE OF THE ANGLE BISECTOR THEOREM

If a point is in the interior of an angle and is equidistant from the _____ of the angle, then it lies on the bisector of the angle.

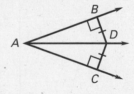

If ____ = ____, then $m\angle BAD = m\angle CAD$.

Example 2 *Using Angle Bisectors*

Baseball Field Use the diagram of the baseball infield shown at the right. What can you conclude about the measure of ∠SHF?

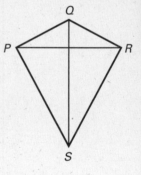

Second base, S

Pitcher's mound, M

Third base, T

First base, F

Home, H

Solution

From the diagram, you know that point ___ is in the interior of ∠THF and ST = ___.

From the _____ _____ Theorem, you know that S lies on the angle bisector of ∠ ___. An angle bisector divides an angle into two congruent angles, each of which has ___ the measure of the original angle, so

m∠SHF = _____ = ___°.

Answer The measure of ∠SHF is ___°.

✔ Checkpoint Complete the following exercises.

1. In the diagram, $\overline{PQ} \cong \overline{RQ}$. What conclusion can you make about point Q? Can you conclude that S is on the perpendicular bisector of $\overline{PR}$? Explain.

Q

P   R

S

---

2. In the diagram, D is on the bisector of ∠ABC. What is DC? Explain.

B

8

A   C

6

D

5.2 Bisectors of a Triangle

Goals • Use properties of perpendicular bisectors of a triangle.
• Use properties of angle bisectors of a triangle.

VOCABULARY

Perpendicular bisector of a triangle

Concurrent lines

Point of concurrency

Circumcenter of a triangle

Angle bisector of a triangle

Incenter of a triangle

THEOREM 5.5: CONCURRENCY OF PERPENDICULAR BISECTORS OF A TRIANGLE

The perpendicular bisectors of a triangle
intersect at a point that is _____
from the vertices of the triangle.

PA = ____ = ____

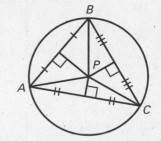

Example 1 **Using Perpendicular Bisectors**

Boating The positions of three boats are shown in the diagram. The boats are equidistant from a buoy. Where is the buoy?

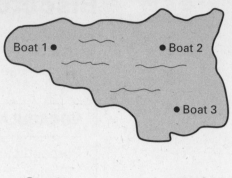

Solution

To find the location of the buoy, find the _____ of the triangle formed by the boats' locations.

Use the diagram at the right to make a sketch that shows the buoy's location. Label the buoy's location.

Boat 1 ●   ● Boat 2

● Boat 3

✔ *Checkpoint* **Complete the following exercise.**

1. The perpendicular bisectors of △*PQR* meet at point *S*. Find *PS* and *QS*.

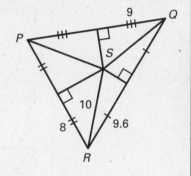

THEOREM 5.6: CONCURRENCY OF ANGLE BISECTORS OF A TRIANGLE

The angle bisectors of a triangle intersect at a point that is equidistant from the sides of the triangle.

PD = _____ = _____

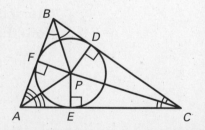

Example 2 **Using Angle Bisectors**

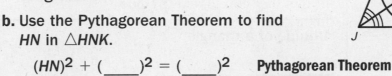

In the diagram, the angle bisectors of
△*JKL* meet at point *H*.

a. What segments are congruent?

b. Find *HN* and *HP*.

Solution

a. By Theorem 5.6, the three angle
bisectors of a triangle intersect at a
point that is equidistant from the sides
of the triangle. So, $HM = HN = HP$.
Therefore, $\overline{HM}$, $\overline{HN}$, and $\overline{HP}$ are
congruent.

b. Use the Pythagorean Theorem to find
HN in △*HNK*.

$(HN)^2 + (\underline{\quad})^2 = (\underline{\quad})^2$	**Pythagorean Theorem**
$(HN)^2 + \underline{\quad}^2 = \underline{\quad}^2$	**Substitute.**
$(HN)^2 + \underline{\quad} = \underline{\quad}$	**Evaluate each square.**
$(HN)^2 = \underline{\quad}$	**Subtract** _____ **from each side.**
$HN = \underline{\quad}$	**Find the positive square root.**

Answer So, $HN = HP = \underline{\quad}$ units.

✔ *Checkpoint* **Complete the following exercise.**

2. The angle bisectors of △*TUV* meet at
point *W*. Find the value of *d*.

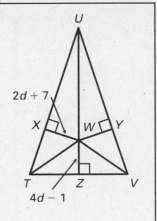

5.3 Medians and Altitudes of a Triangle

Goals • Use properties of medians of a triangle.
• Use properties of altitudes of a triangle.

VOCABULARY

Median of a triangle

Centroid of a triangle

Altitude of a triangle

Orthocenter of a triangle

THEOREM 5.7: CONCURRENCY OF MEDIANS OF A TRIANGLE

The medians of a triangle intersect at a point that is two thirds of the distance from each vertex to the midpoint of the opposite side.

If P is the centroid of $\triangle ABC$, then

$AP = \dfrac{2}{3}$____, $BP = \dfrac{2}{3}$____, and

$CP = \dfrac{2}{3}$____.

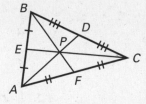

THEOREM 5.8: CONCURRENCY OF ALTITUDES OF A TRIANGLE

The lines containing the altitudes of a triangle are _____.

If $\overline{AE}$, $\overline{BF}$, and $\overline{CD}$ are the altitudes of $\triangle ABC$, then the lines $\overleftrightarrow{AE}$, $\overleftrightarrow{BF}$, and $\overleftrightarrow{CD}$ intersect at some point H.

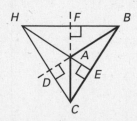

Example 1 *Using the Centroid of a Triangle*

R is the centroid of △*STU* and *SR* = 16. Find *SV* and *RV*.

Solution

Because *R* is the centroid, *SR* = ___ *SV*.

___ = ___ *SV*   **Substitute for SR.**

___ = *SV*   **Simplify.**

By the Segment Addition Postulate, ___ + ___ = *SV*.

___ + *RV* = ___   **Substitute for SR and SV.**

RV = ___   **Simplify.**

Answer So, *SV* = ___ and *RV* = ___.

Example 2 *Finding the Centroid of a Triangle*

Find the coordinates of centroid *C* of △*DEF*.

Solution

You know that the centroid is two thirds of the distance from each vertex to the midpoint of the opposite side.

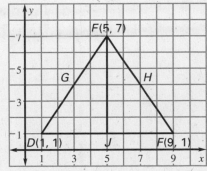

> Use the Midpoint Formula to find the coordinates of *J*.

Choose the median $\overline{EJ}$. Find the coordinates of *J*, the midpoint of $\overline{DF}$. The coordinates of *J* are:

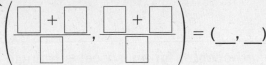

$$\left(\frac{\square + \square}{\square}, \frac{\square + \square}{\square}\right) = (\_\_ , \_\_)$$

Find the distance from vertex *E* to midpoint *J*. The distance from *E* to *J* is ___ − ___, or ___ units.

Determine the coordinates of centroid *C*, which is ___ • ___, or ___ units up from point *J* along the median $\overline{EJ}$.

Answer The coordinates of centroid *C* are (___, ___ + ___), or (___, ___).

Example 3 *Drawing Altitudes and Orthocenters*

Is the orthocenter for △ABC located *inside*, *outside*, or *on* the triangle?

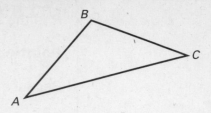

Solution

The orthocenter of △ABC is the intersection of the lines containing the altitudes of the triangle.

Use the diagram at the right to locate the orthocenter D.

Answer So, the orthocenter is located _____ △ABC.

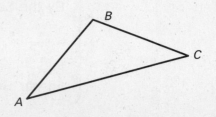

✔ *Checkpoint* **Complete the following exercises.**

1. *T* is the centroid of △QRS and *TU* = 7. Find *QU* and *QT*.

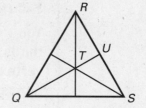

2. Is the orthocenter for an isosceles triangle *always* located inside the triangle? Explain.

5.4 Midsegment Theorem

Goals
- Identify the midsegments of a triangle.
- Use properties of midsegments of a triangle.

VOCABULARY

Midsegment of a triangle

Example 1 *Using Midsegments*

Show that the midsegment $\overline{FG}$ is parallel to side $\overline{CD}$ and is half as long as $\overline{CD}$.

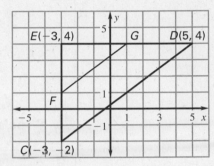

Solution

Use the Midpoint Formula to find the coordinates of F and G.

$$F = \left(\underline{\hspace{3cm}} , \underline{\hspace{3cm}} \right) = (\underline{\hspace{0.8cm}} , \underline{\hspace{0.6cm}})$$

$$G = \left(\underline{\hspace{2cm}} , \underline{\hspace{1.5cm}} \right) = (\underline{\hspace{0.4cm}} , \underline{\hspace{0.4cm}})$$

Next, find the slopes of $\overline{CD}$ and $\overline{FG}$.

Remember: The slope m of the line passing through (x_1, y_1) and (x_2, y_2) is
$$m = \frac{y_2 - y_1}{x_2 - x_1}.$$

Slope of $\overline{CD} = \underline{\hspace{1.5cm}} = \underline{\hspace{1cm}}$

Slope of $\overline{FG} = \underline{\hspace{1.5cm}} =$

▶ Because the slopes are $\underline{\hspace{1.5cm}}$, $\overline{FG}$ is parallel to $\overline{CD}$.

Next, find the lengths of $\overline{CD}$ and $\overline{FG}$.

Use the Distance Formula to find the lengths.

$$CD = \sqrt{[\underline{\hspace{0.4cm}} - (\underline{\hspace{0.4cm}})]^2 + [\underline{\hspace{0.4cm}} - (\underline{\hspace{0.4cm}})]^2} = \sqrt{\underline{\hspace{0.6cm}}} = \underline{\hspace{0.5cm}}$$

$$FG = \sqrt{[\underline{\hspace{0.4cm}} - (\underline{\hspace{0.4cm}})]^2 + (\underline{\hspace{0.4cm}} - \underline{\hspace{0.4cm}})^2} = \sqrt{\underline{\hspace{0.6cm}}} = \underline{\hspace{0.4cm}}$$

▶ Because $\dfrac{FG}{CD} = \underline{\hspace{1cm}} = \underline{\hspace{1cm}}$, $\overline{FG}$ is half as long as $\overline{CD}$.

THEOREM 5.9: MIDSEGMENT THEOREM

The segment connecting the midpoints of
two sides of a triangle is parallel to the
third side and is half as long.

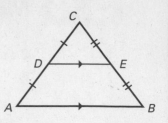

$\overline{DE} \parallel$ ____ and $DE = \dfrac{1}{2}$ ____

Example 2 *Using the Midsegment Theorem*

$\overline{ST}$ and $\overline{TU}$ are midsegments of $\triangle PQR$.
Find PR and ST.

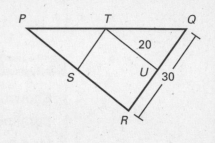

Solution

$PR = 2(\underline{}) = 2(\underline{}) = \underline{}$

$ST = \dfrac{1}{2}(\underline{}) = \dfrac{1}{2}(\underline{}) = \underline{}$

✔ *Checkpoint* **Complete the following exercises.**

1. Show that the midsegment $\overline{MN}$ is
   parallel to side $\overline{JK}$ and is half as
   long as $\overline{JK}$.

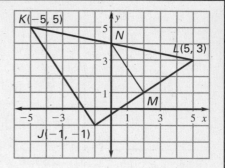

---

2. $\overline{AB}$ and $\overline{BC}$ are midsegments
   of $\triangle XYZ$. Find XZ and BC.

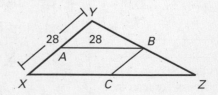

Example 3 *Using Midpoints to Draw a Triangle*

The midpoints of the sides of a triangle are $D(3, 6)$, $E(6, 5)$, and $F(5, 3)$. What are the coordinates of the vertices of the triangle?

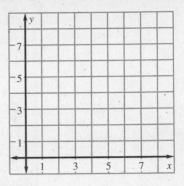

Solution

1. **Plot** the midpoints.

2. **Connect** the midpoints to form $\overline{DE}$, $\overline{EF}$, and $\overline{DF}$.

3. **Find** the slopes of the midsegments.

> Find the slope using the graph and $m = \dfrac{\text{rise}}{\text{run}}$.

Slope of $\overline{DE} = $ _____   Slope of $\overline{EF} = $ __

Slope of $\overline{DF} = $ _____

> Each midsegment contains two of the unknown triangle's midpoints and is parallel to the side that contains the third midpoint. So, you know a point on each side of the triangle and the slope of each side.

4. **Draw** the lines that contain the three sides of the triangle.

5. **Identify** the points at which the lines intersect.

Answer The vertices of the triangle are (__ , __), (__ , __), and (__ , __).

✓ *Checkpoint* **Complete the following exercise.**

3. The midpoints of the sides of a triangle are $D(3, 4)$, $E(5, 8)$, and $F(6, 4)$. What are the coordinates of the vertices of the triangle?

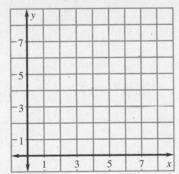

Example 4   *Perimeter of a Triangle*

$\overline{JK}$, $\overline{KL}$, and $\overline{JL}$ are midsegments of
$\triangle MNP$. How does the perimeter of
$\triangle MNP$ compare to the perimeter
of $\triangle JKL$?

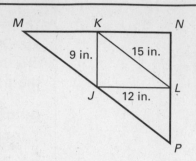

Solution

The lengths of the sides of $\triangle MNP$ are
twice the lengths of the midsegments.

$MP = 2(\_\_\_) = 2(\_\_\_) = \_\_\_$ in.

$MN = 2(\_\_\_) = 2(\_\_\_) = \_\_\_$ in.

$NP = 2(\_\_\_) = 2(\_\_) = \_\_\_$ in.

The perimeter of $\triangle MNP$ is $\_\_\_ + \_\_\_ + \_\_\_ = \_\_\_$ inches.

The perimeter of $\triangle JKL$ is $\_\_\_ + \_\_\_ + \_\_ = \_\_\_$ inches.

Answer The perimeter of $\triangle MNP$ is _____ the perimeter of $\triangle JKL$.

✔ *Checkpoint* **Complete the following exercise.**

4. $\overline{DE}$, $\overline{EF}$, and $\overline{DF}$ are midsegments of $\triangle ABC$. Find the perimeters
of $\triangle ABC$ and $\triangle DEF$. How does the perimeter of $\triangle DEF$ compare
to the perimeter of $\triangle ABC$?

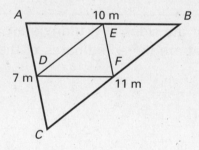

5.5 Inequalities in One Triangle

Goals • Use triangle measurements to decide which side is longest or which angle is largest.
• Use the Triangle Inequality.

THEOREM 5.10

If one side of a triangle is longer than another side, then the angle opposite the longer side is _____ than the angle opposite the shorter side.

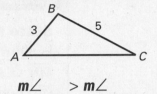

$m\angle\_\_\_ > m\angle\_\_\_$

THEOREM 5.11

If one angle of a triangle is larger than another angle, then the side opposite the larger angle is _____ than the side opposite the smaller angle.

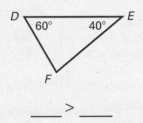

$\_\_\_ > \_\_\_$

Example 1   *Writing Measurements in Order from Least to Greatest*

Write the measures of the triangles in order from least to greatest.

a.

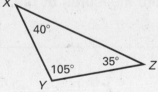

b.

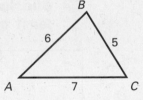

Solution

a. $m\angle\_\_\_ < m\angle\_\_\_ < m\angle\_\_\_$

$\_\_\_ < \_\_\_ < \_\_\_$

b. $\_\_\_ < \_\_\_ < \_\_\_$

$m\angle\_\_\_ < m\angle\_\_\_ < m\angle\_\_\_$

THEOREM 5.12: EXTERIOR ANGLE INEQUALITY

The measure of an exterior angle of a triangle is greater than the measure of either of the two nonadjacent interior angles.

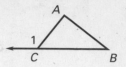

$$m\angle 1 > m\angle \underline{\quad} \text{ and } m\angle 1 > m\angle \underline{\quad}$$

Example 2   *Using Theorem 5.10*

State Flags The state flag of Ohio is shown at the right. In the flag, $\overline{MN} \cong \overline{PN}$ and $MP < MN$. What can you conclude about the angle measures in $\triangle MNP$?

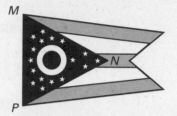

Solution

- Because $\overline{MN} \cong \overline{PN}$, $\triangle MNP$ is _____ . So, $\angle \underline{\quad} \cong \angle \underline{\quad}$. Therefore, $m\angle \underline{\quad} = m\angle \underline{\quad}$.

- By Theorem 5.10, because $MP < MN$, $m\angle \underline{\quad} < m\angle \underline{\quad}$.

- Because $\overline{MN} \cong \overline{PN}$, $MN = PN$. So, by substitution, $\underline{\quad} < PN$. By Theorem 5.10, $m\angle \underline{\quad} < m\angle \underline{\quad}$.

- In addition, you can conclude that $m\angle M \underline{\quad} 60°$, $m\angle N \underline{\quad} 60°$, and $m\angle P \underline{\quad} 60°$.

> The sum of the angle measures in a triangle is 180°. In $\triangle MNP$, use logical reasoning to decide whether an angle measure is less than 60° or greater than 60°.

✔ *Checkpoint* Write the measures of the triangle in order from least to greatest.

1.

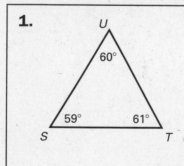

2.

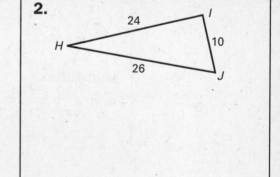

THEOREM 5.13: TRIANGLE INEQUALITY

The sum of the lengths of any two sides of a triangle is greater than the length of the third side.

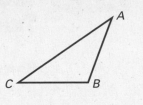

____ + ____ > *AC*

AC + ____ > ____

____ + *AC* > ____

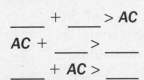 **Finding Possible Side Lengths**

A triangle has one side of 12 inches and another side of 20 inches. Describe the possible lengths of the third side.

Solution

Let *x* represent the length of the third side. Using the Triangle Inequality, you can write and solve inequalities.

x + ___ > ___   ___ + ___ > *x*

      x > ___   ___ > *x*

Answer The length of the third side must be greater than ___ inches and less than ___ inches.

✓ *Checkpoint* Decide if it is possible to construct a triangle having the given side lengths. If it is not possible, explain.

3. 13 mm, 25 mm, 14 mm	4. 9 in., 17 in., 8 in.

5. A triangle has one side of 8 millimeters and another side of 11 millimeters. Describe the possible lengths of the third side.

5.6 Indirect Proof and Inequalities in Two Triangles

Goals • Read and write an indirect proof.
• Use the Hinge Theorem and its converse to compare side lengths and angle measures.

VOCABULARY

Indirect proof

THEOREM 5.14: HINGE THEOREM

If two sides of one triangle are congruent to two sides of another triangle, and the included angle of the first is larger than the included angle of the second, then the third side of the first is _____ than the third side of the second.

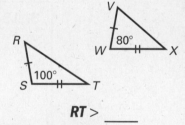

$RT >$ _____

THEOREM 5.15: CONVERSE OF THE HINGE THEOREM

If two sides of one triangle are congruent to two sides of another triangle, and the third side of the first is longer than the third side of the second, then the included angle of the first is _____ than the included angle of the second.

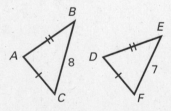

$m\angle A > m\angle$ ____

GUIDELINES FOR WRITING AN INDIRECT PROOF

1. Identify the statement that you want to prove is _____ .

2. Begin by assuming the statement is _____ ; assume the opposite is _____ .

3. Obtain statements that logically follow from the _____ .

4. If you obtain a contradiction, then the original statement must be _____ .

Example 1   *Using Indirect Proof*

Use an indirect proof to prove that a right triangle cannot have an obtuse angle.

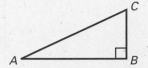

Solution

Given: $\triangle ABC$ is a right triangle with $m\angle B = 90°$.

Prove: $\triangle ABC$ does not have an obtuse angle.

Begin by assuming that _____ .

$m\angle A > \underline{\quad}°$ **Assumption**

$m\angle A + m\angle B > \underline{\quad}°$ **Add angle measures.**

The sum of the measures of all *three* angles is _____° .

$m\angle A + m\angle B + m\angle C = \underline{\quad}°$ **Triangle Sum Theorem**

$m\angle A + m\angle B = 180° - \underline{\quad}$ **Subtraction property of equality**

Substitute $180° - m\angle C$ for $m\angle A + m\angle B$.

$180° - m\angle C \underline{\quad} 180°$ **Substitution property of equality**

$\underline{\quad} > m\angle C$ **Simplify.**

The last statement is not possible because angle measures in triangles cannot be _____ . So, you can conclude that the _____ must be false and that a right triangle _____ _____ .

Example 2 *Finding Possible Side Lengths and Angle Measures*

You can use the Hinge Theorem and its converse to choose possible side lengths or angle measures from a given list.

a. Which of the following is a possible length for $\overline{MN}$: 16 cm, 19 cm, or 22 cm?

b. Which of the following is a possible measure for $\angle C$: 15°, 20°, or 25°?

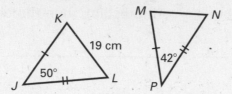

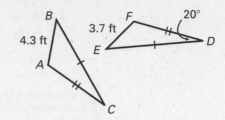

Solution

a. Because the included angle in $\triangle JKL$ is larger than the included angle in $\triangle MNP$, the third side $\overline{KL}$ must be _____ than $\overline{MN}$.

So, of the three choices, the only possible length for $\overline{MN}$ is ____ centimeters.

b. Because the third side in $\triangle ABC$ is longer than the third side in $\triangle DEF$, the included $\angle C$ must be _____ than $\angle D$. So, of the three choices, the only possible measure for $\angle C$ is ____°.

✔ *Checkpoint* **Complete the statement with < or >.**

1. *AB* ___ *YZ*

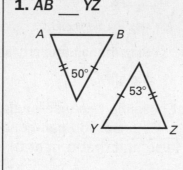

2. $m\angle 1$ ___ $m\angle 2$

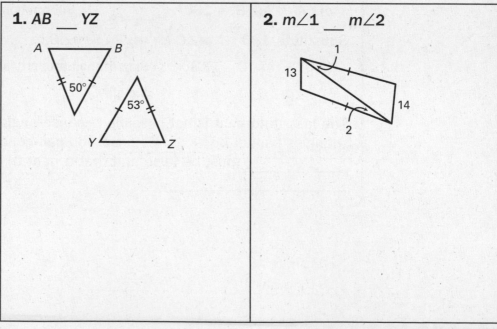

Words to Review

Give an example of the vocabulary word.

Perpendicular bisector	Equidistant from two points
Distance from a point to a line	Equidistant from two lines
Perpendicular bisector of a triangle	Concurrent lines
Point of concurrency	Circumcenter of a triangle

Angle bisector of a triangle	Incenter of a triangle
Median of a triangle	Centroid of a triangle
Altitude of a triangle	Orthocenter of a triangle
Midsegment of a triangle	Indirect proof

Review your notes and Chapter 5 by using the Chapter Review on pages 310–312 of your textbook.

6.1 Polygons

Goals • Identify, name, and describe polygons.
• Use the sum of the measures of the interior angles of a quadrilateral.

VOCABULARY

Polygon

Sides

Vertex

Convex

Nonconvex

Concave

Equilateral

Equiangular

Regular

Diagonal

Example 1   *Identifying Polygons*

State whether the figure is a polygon. If it is not, explain why.

     E

Solution

Figures ___ and ___ are polygons.

• Figure ___ is not a polygon because _____
  _____.

• Figure ___ is not a polygon because _____
  _____.

• Figure ___ is not a polygon because _____
  _____.

Example 2   *Identifying Convex and Concave Polygons*

Identify the polygon and state whether it is convex or concave.

a.   b.

Solution

a. The polygon has ___ sides, so it is a
   _____. When extended, none
   of the sides intersect the interior, so
   the polygon is _____.

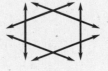

b. The polygon has ___ sides, so it is a
   _____. When extended, some
   of the sides intersect the interior, so
   the polygon is _____.

Example 3 *Identifying Regular Polygons*

Decide whether the polygon is regular.

a. 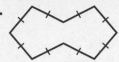   b. 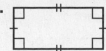   c.

Solution

a. The polygon is _____ , but it is not _____ . So, it
   _____ regular.

b. The polygon is _____ , but it is not _____ . So, it
   _____ regular.

c. The polygon is _____ and _____ . So, it _____
   regular.

✔ *Checkpoint* **Name the polygon. Is the polygon convex or
concave? Is it regular?**

1.	2.	3.

THEOREM 6.1: INTERIOR ANGLES OF A QUADRILATERAL

The sum of the measures of the interior
angles of a quadrilateral is _____°.

$$m\angle 1 + m\angle 2 + m\angle 3 + m\angle 4 = \underline{\qquad}°$$

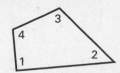

Example 4 *Interior Angles of a Quadrilateral*

Find *m∠U* and *m∠V*.

Solution

Find the value of *x*. Use the sum of the measures of the interior angles to write an equation involving *x*. Then, solve the equation.

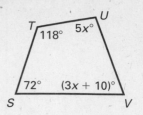

$5x° + (3x + 10)° + 72° + 118° =$ _____ °   Use Theorem 6.1.

_____ + _____ = _____   **Combine like terms.**

_____ = _____   **Subtract** _____ **from each side.**

$x =$ _____   **Divide each side by __.**

Find *m∠U* and *m∠V*.

$m∠U = 5x° = (5 ·$ _____ $)° =$ _____ °

$m∠V = (3x + 10)° = (3 ·$ _____ $+ 10)° =$ _____ °

Answer So, *m∠U* = _____ ° and *m∠V* = _____ °.

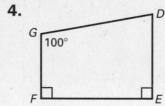 **Checkpoint** Find *m∠D*.

4.	5.
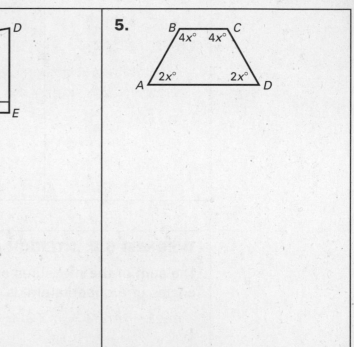	

6.2 Properties of Parallelograms

Goals • Use some properties of parallelograms.
• Use properties of parallelograms in real-life situations.

VOCABULARY

Parallelogram

THEOREM 6.2

If a quadrilateral is a parallelogram, then
its **opposite sides** are congruent.

_____ $\cong \overline{RS}$ and $\overline{SP} \cong$ _____

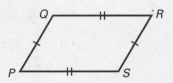

THEOREM 6.3

If a quadrilateral is a parallelogram, then
its **opposite angles** are congruent.

$\angle P \cong \angle$___ and $\angle$___ $\cong \angle S$

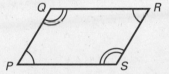

THEOREM 6.4

If a quadrilateral is a parallelogram, then
its **consecutive angles** are supplementary.

$m\angle P + m\angle Q =$ _____°,
$m\angle Q + m\angle R =$ _____°,
$m\angle R + m\angle S =$ _____°,
$m\angle S + m\angle P =$ _____°

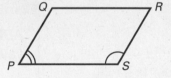

THEOREM 6.5

If a quadrilateral is a parallelogram, then
its diagonals **bisect** each other.

$\overline{QM} \cong$ _____ and _____ $\cong \overline{RM}$

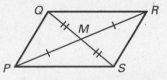

Example 1   *Using Properties of Parallelograms*

STUV is a parallelogram. Find the
unknown length.

a. TU   b. WT

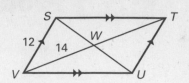

Solution

a. TU = ____   Opposite sides of a ▱ are ≅ .

  TU = ___   Substitute ___ for ____.

b. WT = ____   Diagonals of a ▱ bisect each other.

  WT = ___   Substitute ___ for ____.

Example 2   *Using Properties of Parallelograms*

JKLM is a parallelogram. Find m∠L.

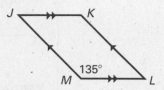

Solution

m∠L + m∠ ___ = ____°   Consecutive angles of a ▱ are
                            supplementary.

m∠L + ____° = ____°   Substitute ____° for m∠___.

m∠L = ___°   Subtract ____° from each side.

Example 3   *Using Algebra with Parallelograms*

ABCD is a parallelogram. Find the
value of x.

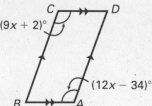

Solution

m∠___ = m∠___   Opposite angles of a ▱ are ≅.

____ + __ = ____ − ____   Substitute.

____ + ___ = ____   Add ___ to each side.

____ = __ x   Subtract ____ from each side.

____ = x   Divide each side by __.

✔ **Checkpoint** Find the measure or value in parallelogram *DEFG*. Explain your reasoning.

1. Find $m\angle D$.

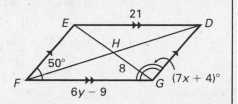

2. Find *EH*.

3. Find the value of *y* in the parallelogram above.

4. Find the value of *x* in the parallelogram above.

Example 4   *Using Parallelograms in Real Life*

Gemstones A gemstone is cut so that one of its facets has four sides. The measures of the consecutive angles in the facet are 45°, 135°, 135°, and 45°. Is the facet a parallelogram? Explain.

Solution

The facet is not a parallelogram. Here are two reasons why.

• The opposite angles _____.

• The sums of the measures of the consecutive angles are _____°, _____°, _____°, and ____°. If the facet were a parallelogram, then all pairs of consecutive angles would be _____ .

6.3 Proving Quadrilaterals are Parallelograms

Goals • Prove that a quadrilateral is a parallelogram.
• Use coordinate geometry with parallelograms.

THEOREM 6.6

If both pairs of opposite _____ of a quadrilateral are congruent, then the quadrilateral is a parallelogram.

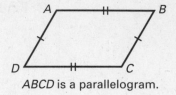

ABCD is a parallelogram.

THEOREM 6.7

If both pairs of opposite _____ of a quadrilateral are congruent, then the quadrilateral is a parallelogram.

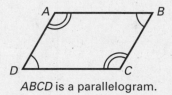

ABCD is a parallelogram.

THEOREM 6.8

If an angle of a quadrilateral is _____ to both of its consecutive angles, then the quadrilateral is a parallelogram.

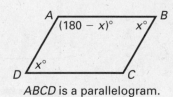

ABCD is a parallelogram.

THEOREM 6.9

If the diagonals of a quadrilateral _____ each other, then the quadrilateral is a parallelogram.

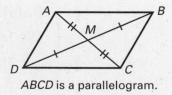

ABCD is a parallelogram.

Example 1 **Proof of Theorem 6.8**

Prove Theorem 6.8.

Given: ∠J is supplementary to ∠K and ∠M.
Prove: JKLM is a parallelogram.

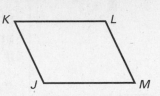

Statements	Reasons
1. ∠J is supplementary to ∠K.	1. Given
2. $\overline{JM}$ ∥ _____	2. _____
	_____
3. ∠J is supplementary to ∠M.	3. Given
4. $\overline{JK}$ ∥ _____	4. _____
	_____
5. JKLM is a parallelogram.	5. _____
	_____

✔ *Checkpoint* **Complete the following exercise.**

1. **Stained Glass** A pane in a stained glass window has the shape shown at the right. How do you know that the pane is a parallelogram?

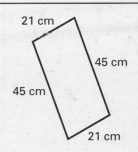

THEOREM 6.10

If one pair of opposite sides of a quadrilateral are _____ and _____, then the quadrilateral is a parallelogram.

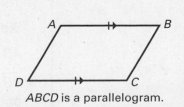

ABCD is a parallelogram.

Example 2 *Using Properties of Parallelograms*

Show that $A(1, 3)$, $B(3, 5)$, $C(9, 1)$, and $D(7, -1)$ are the vertices of a parallelogram.

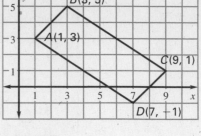

Solution

Method 1 Show that opposite sides have the same slope.

To find the slopes of the opposite sides, use

$$\text{slope} = \frac{\text{rise}}{\text{run}}$$

$$= \frac{y_2 - y_1}{x_2 - x_1}.$$

Slope of $\overline{AB}$:

$$\frac{\boxed{} - 3}{\boxed{} - \boxed{}} = \underline{}$$

Slope of $\overline{BC}$:

$$\frac{\boxed{} - 1}{\boxed{} - \boxed{}} = \underline{}$$

Slope of $\overline{CD}$:

$$\frac{\boxed{} - (-1)}{\boxed{} - \boxed{}} = \underline{}$$

Slope of $\overline{AD}$:

$$\frac{3 - \boxed{}}{\boxed{} - \boxed{}} = \underline{}$$

▶ $\overline{AB}$ and ____ have the same slope, so they are parallel. Similarly, $\overline{BC} \parallel$ ____. Because opposite sides are _____, *ABCD* is a parallelogram.

Method 2 Show that opposite sides have the same length.

To find the lengths of the sides, use the Distance Formula.

$$AB = \sqrt{(\underline{} - 1)^2 + (\underline{} - \underline{})^2} = \sqrt{\underline{}} = \underline{}$$

$$BC = \sqrt{(9 - \underline{})^2 + (\underline{} - \underline{})^2} = \sqrt{\underline{}} = \underline{}$$

$$CD = \sqrt{(\underline{} - 7)^2 + [\underline{} - (\underline{})]^2} = \sqrt{\underline{}} = \underline{}$$

$$AD = \sqrt{(\underline{} - \underline{})^2 + (-1 - \underline{})^2} = \sqrt{\underline{}} = \underline{}$$

▶ $\overline{AB} \cong$ ____ and $\overline{BC} \cong$ ____. Because both pairs of opposite sides are _____, *ABCD* is a parallelogram.

Method 3 Show that one pair of opposite sides is congruent and parallel.

Slope of $\overline{AB}$ = Slope of $\overline{CD}$ = __

$AB = CD =$ _____

▶ $\overline{AB}$ and $\overline{CD}$ are _____ and _____. So, *ABCD* is a parallelogram.

6.4 Rhombuses, Rectangles, and Squares

Goals • Use properties of sides and angles of rhombuses, rectangles, and squares.
• Use properties of diagonals of rhombuses, rectangles, and squares.

VOCABULARY

Rhombus

Rectangle

Square

Example 1   *Describing a Special Parallelogram*

Decide whether the statement is *always*, *sometimes*, or *never* true.

a. A square is a rectangle.

b. A rectangle is a square.

Solution

a. The statement is _____ true. Because all squares have four _____, squares are _____ rectangles.

b. The statement is _____ true. If a rectangle has four congruent _____, then it is also a square.

Example 2 *Using Properties of Special Parallelograms*

ABCD is a rhombus. What else do you know about ABCD?

- ABCD has four congruent _____.
- Its opposite sides are _____.
- Its opposite angles are _____.
- Its diagonals _____.
- Its consecutive angles are _____.

RHOMBUS COROLLARY

A quadrilateral is a rhombus if and only if it has four congruent _____.

RECTANGLE COROLLARY

A quadrilateral is a rectangle if and only if it has four _____.

SQUARE COROLLARY

A quadrilateral is a square if and only if it is a _____ and a _____.

Example 3 *Using Properties of a Rectangle*

In the diagram, *EFGH* is a rectangle. What is the value of *y*?

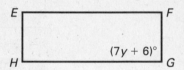

Solution

All four angles of a rectangle are _____. So, $m\angle G =$ ___°.

$(7y + 6)° =$ ___°   Write equation.

$7y =$ ___   Subtract ___ from each side.

$y =$ ___   Divide each side by ___.

1. A rhombus is a square.	**2.** A parallelogram is a rectangle.

3. *QRST* is a square. What is the value of *x*?

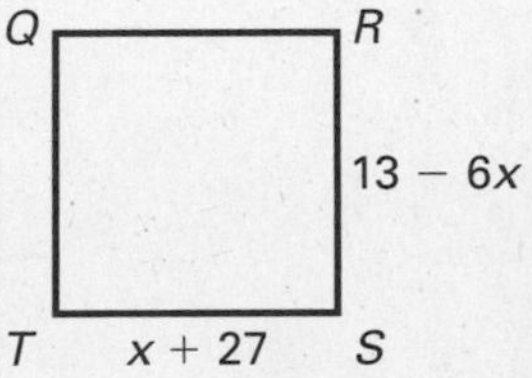

$$13 - 6x$$

$$x + 27$$

THEOREM 6.11

A parallelogram is a rhombus if and only if its diagonals are _____.

ABCD is a rhombus if and only if ____ ⊥ ____.

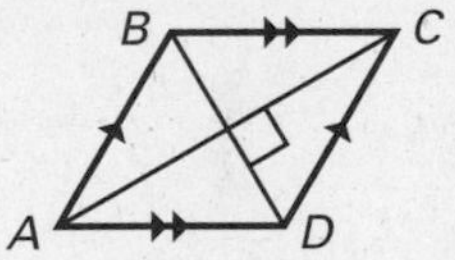

THEOREM 6.12

A parallelogram is a rhombus if and only if each diagonal bisects a pair of opposite angles.

ABCD is a rhombus if and only if

$\overline{AC}$ bisects ∠_____ and ∠_____ and

$\overline{BD}$ bisects ∠_____ and ∠_____.

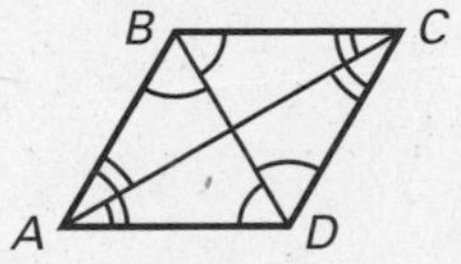

THEOREM 6.13

A parallelogram is a rectangle if and only if its diagonals are _____.

ABCD is a rectangle if and only if

____ ≅ ____.

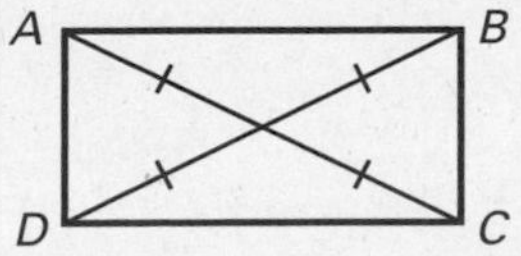

Example 4 *Checking a Square*

Tree House You are building a tree house.

a. To make the base of the floor, you nail four pieces of wood together as shown at the right. What is the shape of the floor base? Explain.

b. To make sure the base is a square, you measure the length of the diagonals. Both diagonals measure 11 feet 4 inches. Is the base a square? Explain.

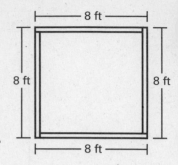

Solution

a. All four sides are _____ . So, the floor base is a _____ .

b. The diagonals are _____ . So, the floor base is a _____ . Because the base is a rhombus and a _____ , it is also a _____ .

✔ *Checkpoint* **Decide whether the statement is *true* or *false*. Explain your reasoning.**

4. The diagonals of a rhombus are always congruent.

5. The diagonals of a square are never perpendicular.

6. Each diagonal of a rectangle sometimes bisects a pair of opposite angles.

6.5 Trapezoids and Kites

Goals • Use properties of trapezoids.
• Use properties of kites.

VOCABULARY

Trapezoid

Bases of a trapezoid

Base angles of a trapezoid

Legs of a trapezoid

Isosceles trapezoid

Midsegment of a trapezoid

Kite

THEOREM 6.14

If a trapezoid is isosceles, then each pair of base angles is _____.

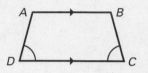

$\angle A \cong \angle \underline{\hspace{0.5cm}}, \angle \underline{\hspace{0.5cm}} \cong \angle D$

THEOREM 6.15

If a trapezoid has a pair of congruent _____, then it is an isosceles trapezoid.

ABCD is an isosceles trapezoid.

THEOREM 6.16

A trapezoid is isosceles if and only if its diagonals are _____.

ABCD is isosceles if and only

if _____ $\cong$ _____.

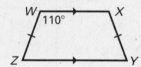

Example 1 *Using Properties of Isosceles Trapezoids*

WXYZ is an isosceles trapezoid. Find *m∠X*, *m∠Y*, and *m∠Z*.

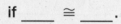

Solution

• *WXYZ* is an isosceles trapezoid, so *m∠X = m∠____ = ____°*.

• ∠W and ∠Z are consecutive interior angles formed by parallel lines, so they are _____.

    m∠W + m∠Z = ____°   **Consecutive Interior Angles Theorem**

    ____° + *m∠Z* = ____°   **Substitute for *m∠W*.**

    m∠Z = ____°   **Subtract ____° from each side.**

• *WXYZ* is an isosceles trapezoid, so *m∠Y = m∠____ = ____°*.

Example 2   *Using Properties of Trapezoids*

Show that *HIJK* is a trapezoid.

Compare the slopes of opposite sides.

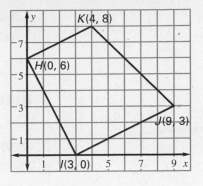

Slope of $\overline{HK}$ = _____ = ___ = ___

Slope of $\overline{IJ}$ = _____ = ___ = ___

The slopes of $\overline{HK}$ and $\overline{IJ}$ are equal,
so $\overline{HK} \parallel \overline{IJ}$.

Slope of $\overline{HI}$ = _____ = ___ = ___

Slope of $\overline{JK}$ = _____ = ___ = ___

The slopes of $\overline{HI}$ and $\overline{JK}$ are not equal, so $\overline{HI}$ is not parallel to $\overline{JK}$.

Answer Because $\overline{HK} \parallel \overline{IJ}$ and $\overline{HI}$ is not parallel to $\overline{JK}$, *HIJK* is a

_____ .

THEOREM 6.17: MIDSEGMENT THEOREM FOR TRAPEZOIDS

The midsegment of a trapezoid is parallel
to each base and its length is one half the
sum of the lengths of the bases.

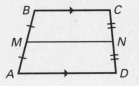

$\overline{MN} \parallel$ ____ , $\overline{MN} \parallel$ ____ , $MN =$ _____

✔ *Checkpoint* Complete the following exercise.

1. *ABCD* is an isosceles trapezoid.
   Find $m\angle A$, $m\angle B$, and $m\angle C$.

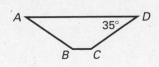

THEOREM 6.18

If a quadrilateral is a kite, then its
diagonals are _____.

_____ ⊥ _____

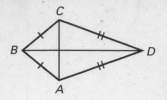

THEOREM 6.19

If a quadrilateral is a kite, then
exactly one pair of opposite angles
are congruent.

∠A ___ ∠C, ∠B ___ ∠D

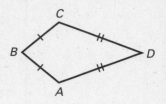

Example 3 *Angles of a Kite*

Find $m\angle S$ and $m\angle U$.

STUV is a kite, so $\angle S \cong \angle$ ___ and
$m\angle S = m\angle$ ___.

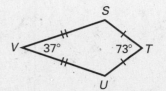

___ $(m\angle S) + m\angle$ ___ $+ m\angle$ ___ $=$ _____° **Sum of measures of int. ∠s of quad. is 360°.**

___ $(m\angle S) +$ ___° $+$ ___° $=$ _____° **Substitute.**

___ $(m\angle S) =$ _____° **Simplify.**

$m\angle S =$ _____° **Divide each side by ___.**

Answer So, $m\angle S = m\angle$ ___ $=$ _____°.

✔ *Checkpoint* Complete the following exercise.

2. Find $m\angle X$ and $m\angle Z$.

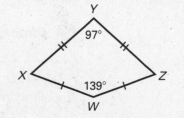

6.6 Special Quadrilaterals

Goals • Identify special quadrilaterals based on limited information.
• Prove that a quadrilateral is a special type of quadrilateral.

Example 1   *Identifying Quadrilaterals*

Quadrilateral *ABCD* has diagonals that are perpendicular. What types of quadrilaterals meet this condition?

Solution

There are three types of quadrilaterals that meet this condition. Draw and label each type of quadrilateral.

_____ _____ _____

✔ *Checkpoint* Identify the special quadrilateral. Use the most specific name.

1.	2.	3.

4. A quadrilateral has diagonals that are not congruent. What types of quadrilaterals meet this condition? Draw and label each type of quadrilateral.

Example 2 **Proving a Quadrilateral is an Isosceles Trapezoid**

Show that *QRST* is an isosceles trapezoid.

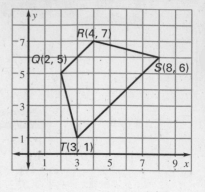

Solution

Here is one way to show that *QRST* is an isosceles trapezoid.

1. Show that *QRST* is a trapezoid by proving $\overline{QR} \parallel$ ____ and $\overline{QT}$ is not parallel to ____.

$$\text{Slope of } \overline{QR} = \frac{\boxed{} - 5}{\boxed{} - \boxed{}} = \underline{}$$

$$\text{Slope of } \overline{ST} = \frac{\boxed{} - \boxed{}}{\boxed{} - 3} = \underline{}$$

$$\text{Slope of } \overline{QT} = \frac{\boxed{} - \boxed{}}{2 - \boxed{}} = \underline{}$$

$$\text{Slope of } \overline{RS} = \frac{7 - \boxed{}}{\boxed{} - \boxed{}} = \underline{}$$

> **Recall that the slopes of parallel lines are equal.**

The slopes of $\overline{QR}$ and ____ are equal, so $\overline{QR} \parallel$ ____. The slopes of $\overline{QT}$ and ____ are not equal. So, these segments are not parallel.

2. Show that *QRST* is isosceles by proving $\overline{QT} \cong$ ____.

$$QT = \sqrt{(\underline{} - 3)^2 + (\underline{} - \underline{})^2}$$
$$= \sqrt{(\underline{})^2 + \underline{}^2}$$
$$= \sqrt{\underline{}}$$

> **Use the Distance Formula to find the lengths of the segments.**

$$\underline{} = \sqrt{(\underline{} - \underline{})^2 + (\underline{} - 6)^2}$$
$$= \sqrt{(\underline{})^2 + \underline{}^2}$$
$$= \sqrt{\underline{}}$$

Because $QT =$ ____, $\overline{QT} \cong$ ____.

Answer Because *QRST* is a quadrilateral with exactly one pair of parallel _____, it is a trapezoid. Because its _____ are congruent, *QRST* is an isosceles trapezoid.

Example 3 *Identifying a Quadrilateral*

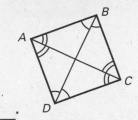

What type of quadrilateral is *ABCD*? Explain your reasoning.

> Use the Alternate Interior Angles Converse to make these conclusions.

Solution

$\angle BAC \cong \angle ACD$, so you can conclude that _____. Similarly, $\angle ADB \cong \angle DBC$, so _____.

- Because *ABCD* is a quadrilateral with both pairs of opposite sides parallel, *ABCD* is a _____.

- Because *ABCD* is a parallelogram and each diagonal bisects a pair of opposite angles, *ABCD* is a _____.

✔ **Checkpoint** **Complete the following exercises.**

---

5. In Example 3, can you conclude that *ABCD* is a square? Explain.

---

6. What type of quadrilateral is *ABCD*? Explain how to prove it.

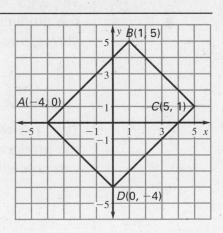

6.7 Areas of Triangles and Quadrilaterals

Goals
- Find the areas of squares, rectangles, parallelograms, and triangles.
- Find the areas of trapezoids, kites, and rhombuses.

POSTULATE 22: AREA OF A SQUARE POSTULATE

The area of a square is the square of the length of its side, or $A =$ ___ .

POSTULATE 23: AREA CONGRUENCE POSTULATE

If two polygons are _____ , then they have the same area.

POSTULATE 24: AREA ADDITION POSTULATE

The area of a region is the _____ of the areas of its nonoverlapping parts.

THEOREM 6.20: AREA OF A RECTANGLE

The area of a rectangle is the product of its base and height.

$A =$ ___

THEOREM 6.21: AREA OF A PARALLELOGRAM

The area of a parallelogram is the product of a base and its corresponding height.

$A =$ ___

THEOREM 6.22: AREA OF A TRIANGLE

The area of a triangle is one half the product of a base and its corresponding height.

$A =$ _____

Example 1 *Using the Area Theorems*

Find the area of □ABCD.

Solution

Use $\overline{AB}$ as the base. So, $b =$ ___ and $h =$ ___.

Area $= bh$

= ___(___)

= ____ square units

Notice that you get the same area using $\overline{BC}$ as the base.

Example 2 *Finding the Height of a Triangle*

Rewrite the formula for the area of a triangle in terms of h. Then use your formula to find the height of a triangle that has an area of 18 and a base length of 6.

Solution

Rewrite the area formula so h is alone on one side of the equation.

$A = $ ____   **Formula for the area of a triangle**

____ = ____   **Multiply each side by 2.**

____ $= h$ **Divide each side by b.**

Substitute ___ for A and ___ for b to find the height of the triangle.

$h = $ ____ $=$ ____ $=$ __

Answer The height of the triangle is __.

✔ **Checkpoint** Find the area or height of the polygon.

1.	2.	3.
8 4	16 9	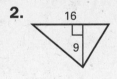 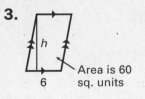

THEOREM 6.23: AREA OF A TRAPEZOID

The area of a trapezoid is one half the product of the height and the sum of the bases.

A = _____

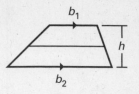

THEOREM 6.24: AREA OF A KITE

The area of a kite is one half the product of the lengths of its diagonals.

A = _____

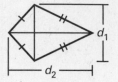

THEOREM 6.25: AREA OF A RHOMBUS

The area of a rhombus is one half the product of the lengths of the diagonals.

A = _____

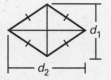

Example 3   *Finding the Area of a Trapezoid*

Find the area of trapezoid *JKLM*.

Solution

The height of *JKLM* is

$h =$ ___ $-$ ___ $=$ ___.

Find the lengths of the bases.

$b_1 = JK =$ ___ $-$ ___ $=$ ___

$b_2 = LM =$ ___ $-$ ___ $=$ ___

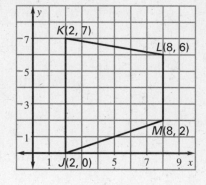

Substitute ___ for h, ___ for b_1, and ___ for b_2 to find the area of the trapezoid.

$A = \frac{1}{2}h(b_1 + b_2)$ **Formula for area of a trapezoid**

$= \frac{1}{2}($___$)($___ $+$ ___$)$ **Substitute.**

$=$ ____   **Simplify.**

Answer The area of trapezoid *JKLM* is ___ square units.

Example 4   *Finding the Area of a Rhombus*

Use the information in the diagram to
find the area of rhombus *ABCD*.

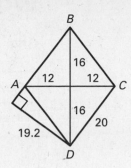

Solution

Method 1 Use the formula for the
area of a rhombus. Let $d_1 = BD =$ ____
and $d_2 = AC =$ ____.

$A =$ ___ $d_1 d_2$

   $=$ ___ (___)(___)

   $=$ ____ square units

Method 2 Use the formula for the area of a parallelogram.
Let $b =$ ___ and $h =$ ____.

$A = bh$

  $= ($___$)($____$)$

  $=$ ____ square units

✔ **Checkpoint** Find the area of the polygon.

4.	5. 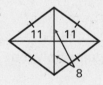	6. 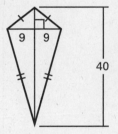

Words to Review

Give an example of the vocabulary word.

Polygon	Sides of a polygon
Vertex	Convex
Nonconvex, concave	Equilateral polygon
Equiangular polygon	Regular polygon
Diagonal of a polygon	Parallelogram

Rhombus	Rectangle
Square	**Trapezoid**
Bases of a trapezoid	**Base angles of a trapezoid**
Legs of a trapezoid	**Isosceles trapezoid**
Midsegment of a trapezoid	**Kite**

Review your notes and Chapter 6 by using the Chapter Review on pages 382–384 of your textbook.

7.1 Rigid Motion in a Plane

Goals • Identify the three basic rigid transformations.
• Use transformations in real-life situations.

VOCABULARY

Image

Preimage

Transformation

Isometry

Example 1 *Naming Transformations*

Use the graph of the transformation at the right.

a. Name and describe the transformation.

b. Name the coordinates of the vertices of the image.

c. Is △*ABC* congruent to its image?

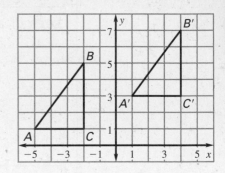

Solution

a. The transformation is a _____ . You can imagine that the image was obtained by sliding △*ABC* up and to the _____ .

b. The coordinates of the vertices of the image, △*A′B′C′*, are
   A′(__ , __), *B′*(__ , __), and *C′*(__ , __).

c. Yes, △*ABC* is congruent to its image △*A′B′C′*. One way to show this would be to use the Distance Formula to find the lengths of the sides of both triangles. Then use the _____ _____ .

> When you name an image, take the corresponding point of the preimage and add a prime symbol. For instance, if the preimage is *A*, the image is *A′*, read as "*A* prime."

✔ **Checkpoint** Name and describe the transformation. Is △*ABC* congruent to its image?

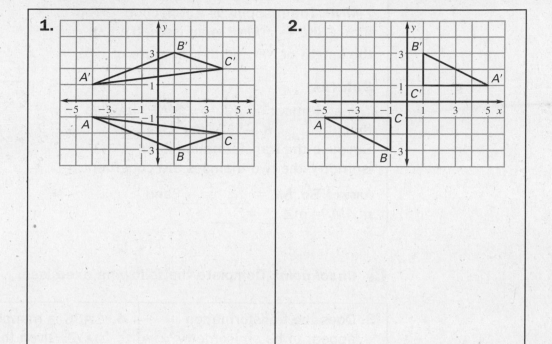

Example 2   *Identifying Isometries*

Does the transformation appear to be an isometry?

a.   b.   c.

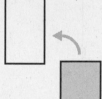   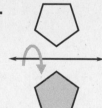   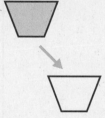

Solution

a. _____. The image is not congruent to the preimage.

b. _____. The shaded pentagon is reflected in a line to produce a congruent unshaded pentagon.

c. _____. The shaded trapezoid is translated down and to the right to form a congruent unshaded trapezoid.

Example 3   *Preserving Length and Angle Measures*

In the diagram, △*JKL* is mapped onto △*MNP*. The mapping is a reflection. Given that △*JKL* → △*MNP* is an isometry, find the length of $\overline{NP}$ and the measure of ∠*M*.

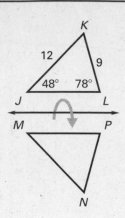

Solution

The statement "△*JKL* → △*MNP*" implies that *J* → ____ , *K* → ____ , and *L* → ____ . Because the transformation is an isometry, the two triangles are congruent.

Answer So, *NP* = ____ = ____ and

m∠*M* = *m*∠____ = ____°.

✔ *Checkpoint* **Complete the following exercises.**

3. Does the transformation appear to be an isometry? Explain. 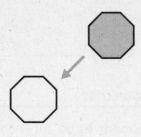	**4.** △*ABC* is mapped onto △*XYZ*. Given that △*ABC* → △*XYZ* is an isometry, find *XZ* and *m*∠*Y*. 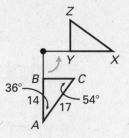

7.2 Reflections

Goals • Identify reflections in a plane.
• Identify relationships between reflections and line symmetry.

VOCABULARY

Reflection

Line of reflection

Line of symmetry

Example 1   *Reflections in a Coordinate Plane*

Graph the given reflection.

a. $J(3, 8)$ in the y-axis

b. $K(7, 4)$ in the line $x = 7$

Solution

a. Because J is ___ units to the right of the y-axis, its reflection, J', is ___ units to the left of the y-axis. Graph and label J'.

b. Graph and label K and the line $x = 7$. Because K is on the line, this implies that $K = $ ___.

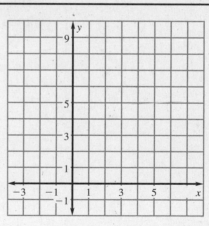

REFLECTIONS IN THE COORDINATE AXES

1. If (x, y) is reflected in the x-axis, its image is the point (___ , _____).

2. If (x, y) is reflected in the y-axis, its image is the point (_____ , ___).

THEOREM 7.1: REFLECTION THEOREM

A reflection is an _____.

Example 2 *Finding Lines of Symmetry*

How many lines of symmetry does the figure have?

a.   b.   c.

Solution

a.   b.    c.

This oval has _____ lines of symmetry.

This pentagon has _____ lines of symmetry.

This octagon has _____ lines of symmetry.

✓ *Checkpoint* **Graph the given reflection in the coordinate plane. Label each image.**

1. $A(0, 2)$ in the x-axis
2. $B(5, 1)$ in the y-axis
3. $C(-4, 3)$ in the line $x = -3$
4. $D(4, 0)$ in the line $y = 2$

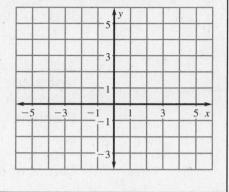

Determine the number of lines of symmetry that the figure has.

5.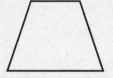

6.

7.

7.3 Rotations

Goals • Identify rotations in a plane.
• Determine whether a figure has rotational symmetry.

VOCABULARY

Rotation

Center of rotation

Angle of rotation

Rotational symmetry

THEOREM 7.2: ROTATION THEOREM

A rotation is an _____.

Example 1 *Rotations in a Coordinate Plane*

Rotate △*ABC* clockwise 90° about the origin and name the coordinates of the new vertices.

△*ABC* is shown in the graph. Use a protractor, a compass, and a straightedge to find the rotated vertices and draw △*A′B′C′*. The coordinates of △*ABC* are listed below. Write the coordinates of △*A′B′C′*.

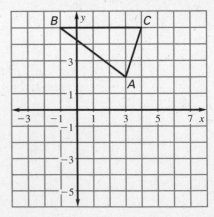

△*ABC*	△*A′B′C′*
A(3, 2)	*A*′(__, ____)
B(−1, 5)	*B*′(__, __)
C(4, 5)	*C*′(__, ____)

✔ **Checkpoint** Name the coordinates of the vertices of the image after the given rotation of △ABC about the origin.

1. 90° clockwise

_____

2. 90° counterclockwise

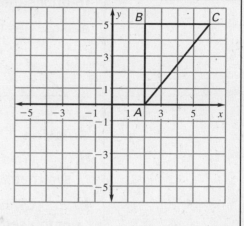

THEOREM 7.3

If lines k and m intersect at point P, then a reflection in k followed by a reflection in m is a rotation about point P.

The angle of rotation is _____°, where $x°$ is the measure of the acute or right angle formed by k and m.

$m\angle BPB'' =$ _____°

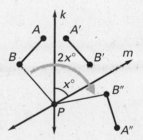

Example 2   **Using Theorem 7.3**

In the diagram, $\overline{HJ}$ is reflected in line k to produce $\overline{H'J'}$. This segment is then reflected in line m to produce $\overline{H''J''}$. Describe the transformation that maps $\overline{HJ}$ to $\overline{H''J''}$.

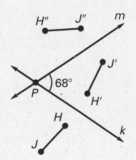

Solution

The acute angle between lines k and m has a measure of _____°. Applying Theorem 7.3, you can conclude that the transformation that maps $\overline{HJ}$ to $\overline{H''J''}$ is a counterclockwise rotation of _____° about point P.

Example 3 | *Identifying Rotational Symmetry*

Does the figure have rotational symmetry? If so, describe the rotations that map the figure onto itself.

a. Isosceles triangle   **b.** Rhombus   **c.** Regular hexagon

Solution

a. ____ . This isosceles triangle _____ rotational symmetry.

b. ____ . This rhombus ____ rotational symmetry. It can be mapped onto itself by a clockwise or counterclockwise rotation of ____° about its center.

c. ____ . This hexagon ____ rotational symmetry. It can be mapped onto itself by a clockwise or counterclockwise rotation of ___°, ____°, or ____° about its center.

✔ **Checkpoint** Does the figure have rotational symmetry? If so, describe the rotations that map the figure onto itself.

3.	4.	5.
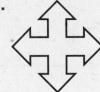	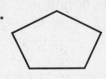	

7.4 Translations and Vectors

Goals • Identify and use translations in the plane.
• Use vectors to describe translations.

VOCABULARY

Translation

_____

Vector

_____

Initial point

_____

Terminal point

_____

Component form

THEOREM 7.4: TRANSLATION THEOREM

A translation is an _____.

THEOREM 7.5

If lines _k_ and _m_ are parallel, then a reflection in line _k_ followed by a reflection in line _m_ is a _____. If _P″_ is the image of _P_, then the following is true:

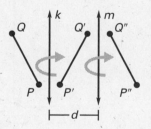

1. $\overleftrightarrow{PP'}$ is _____ to _k_ and _m_.

2. _PP″_ = ____ where _d_ is the distance between _k_ and _m_.

Example 1   *Translations in a Coordinate Plane*

Sketch the image of △*ABC* after the translation
$(x, y) \rightarrow (x + 4, y - 5)$.

Graph △*A'B'C'* by shifting each point
___ units to the _____ and ___ units
_____.

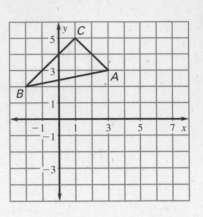

The coordinates of △*ABC* are listed
below. Write the coordinates of
△*A'B'C'*.

△*ABC*	△*A'B'C'*
A(3, 3)	A'(___ , ___)
B(−2, 2)	B'(___ , ___)
C(1, 5)	C'(___ , ___)

✔ *Checkpoint* **Write the coordinates of the vertices of the image
after the given translation of △*ABC*.**

1. $(x, y) \rightarrow (x - 6, y + 3)$

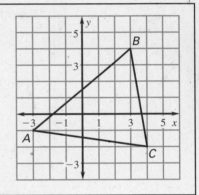

Example 2   *Identifying Vector Components*

Name the vector and write its component form.

a.
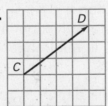

The vector is

_____ = _____ .

b.
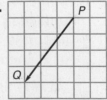

The vector is

_____ = _____ .

Example 3 **Translation Using Vectors**

The component form of $\overrightarrow{JK}$ is $\langle 3, 6 \rangle$. Use $\overrightarrow{JK}$ to translate $\triangle DEF$.

The component form of $\overrightarrow{JK}$ is $\langle 3, 6 \rangle$, so the image vertices should be __ units to the _____ and __ units ____ from the preimage vertices. Graph and label the image vertices. Then use a straightedge to draw $\triangle D'E'F'$.

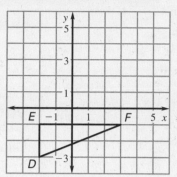

The vertices of $\triangle D'E'F'$ are $D'(\underline{\ }, \underline{\ })$, $E'(\underline{\ }, \underline{\ })$, and $F'(\underline{\ }, \underline{\ })$.

✓ *Checkpoint* **Write the coordinates of the vertices of the image produced by translating $\triangle ABC$ using the given vector.**

2. $\langle -4, 8 \rangle$

_____

3. $\langle 0, -6 \rangle$

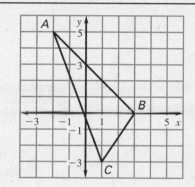

_____

4. $\langle 7, 0 \rangle$

7.5 Glide Reflections and Compositions

Goals • Identify glide reflections in a plane.
• Represent transformations as compositions of simpler transformations.

VOCABULARY

Glide reflection

Composition

| **Example 1** | *Finding the Image of a Glide Reflection* |

Sketch the image of △ABC after a glide reflection.

> **Translation:** $(x, y) \rightarrow (x, y + 8)$
> **Reflection:** in the y-axis

Translate △ABC by moving it ___ units ___ to produce △A'B'C'.
The vertices of △A'B'C' are A'(__, __), B'(__, __), and C'(__, __).
Next, reflect △A'B'C' in the y-axis to produce △A"B"C". Its vertices
are A"(____, __), B"(____, __), and C"(____, __).

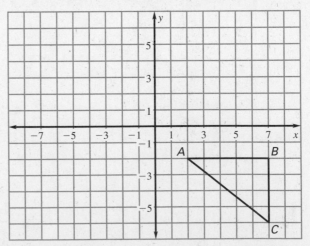

Checkpoint Write the coordinates of the image of $P(4, -2)$ after the given glide reflection.

1. Translation: $(x, y) \to (x + 4, y)$ **Reflection:** in the x-axis	**2. Translation:** $(x, y) \to (x, y - 6)$ **Reflection:** in the y-axis

---

THEOREM 7.6: COMPOSITION THEOREM

The composition of two (or more) Isometries is an Isometry.

Example 2   *Finding the Image of a Composition*

Sketch the image of $\overline{MN}$ after a composition of the given rotation and reflection.

$M(-4, 2)$, $N(-2, 5)$

Rotation: 90° clockwise about the origin

Reflection: in the x-axis

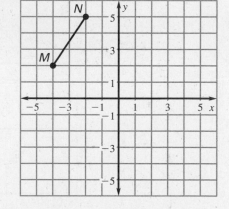

Solution

The graph of $\overline{MN}$ is shown.

Rotate $\overline{MN}$ 90° about the origin to produce $\overline{M'N'}$. The endpoints of $\overline{M'N'}$ are $M'(\underline{\ }, \underline{\ })$ and $N'(\underline{\ }, \underline{\ })$.

Reflect $\overline{M'N'}$ in the x-axis to produce $\overline{M''N''}$. The endpoints of $\overline{M''N''}$ are $M''(\underline{\ }, \underline{\ })$ and $N''(\underline{\ }, \underline{\ })$.

Example 3 *Describing a Composition*

Describe the composition of transformations in the diagram.

Solution

Two transformations are shown. First, △*PQR* is rotated _____° about the origin to produce △*P′Q′R′*. Then △*P′Q′R′* is translated using $(x, y) \rightarrow (\underline{\hspace{1cm}}, \underline{\hspace{1cm}})$ to produce △*P″Q″R″*.

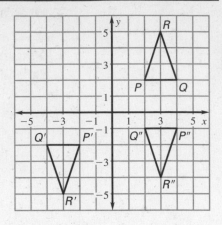

✓ **Checkpoint** Write the coordinates of the image of A(−3, 5) after a composition using the given transformations in the order they appear.

3. Translation: $(x, y) \rightarrow$ $(x + 9, y - 8)$ **Rotation:** 90° counterclockwise about the origin	**4. Rotation:** 180° about the origin **Reflection:** in the y-axis

Describe the composition of the transformations.

5.

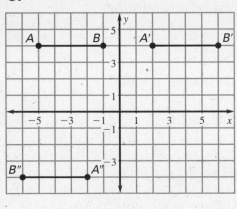

6.

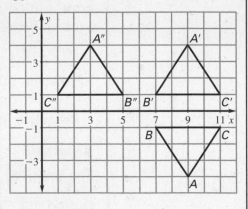

7.6 Frieze Patterns

Goals • Use transformations to classify frieze patterns.
• Use frieze patterns to design border patterns in real life.

VOCABULARY

Frieze pattern

Border pattern

Example 1   *Describing Frieze Patterns*

Describe the transformations that map the frieze pattern onto itself.

a.

b.

c.

Solution

a. This frieze pattern can be mapped onto itself by a _____
_____ (__) or by a _____ (__).

b. This frieze pattern can be mapped onto itself by a _____
_____ (__) or by a _____ (__).

c. This frieze pattern can be mapped onto itself by a _____
_____ (__) or by a _____ (__).

✔ **Checkpoint** Describe the transformations that map the frieze pattern onto itself.

1. ♫♫♫♫♫♫

CLASSIFICATION OF FRIEZE PATTERNS

T	Translation	
TR	Translation and 180° rotation	
TG	Translation and horizontal glide reflection	
TV	Translation and vertical line reflection	
THG	Translation, horizontal line reflection, and horizontal glide reflection	
TRVG	Translation, 180° rotation, vertical line reflection, and horizontal glide reflection	
TRHVG	Translation, 180° rotation, horizontal line reflection, vertical line reflection, and horizontal glide reflection	

Example 2 *Classifying a Frieze Pattern*

Native Americans Categorize the band pattern in the Native American headdress.

Solution

The pattern is a _____.

2.

Example 3   *Drawing a Frieze Pattern*

Tiling A border on a floor is created using the tile shown at the right. The border pattern is classified as TV. Draw one such pattern.

Solution

Begin by reflecting the given tile vertically. Use this tile and the original tile to create a pattern that has a vertical line of symmetry. Then translate the pattern several times to create the frieze pattern.

✔ **Checkpoint** Complete the following exercise.

---

3. Use the tile in Example 3 to draw a pattern that can be classified as TG.

Words to Review

Give an example of the vocabulary word.

Image	Preimage
Transformation	Isometry
Reflection	Line of reflection
Line of symmetry	Rotation
Center of rotation	Angle of rotation

Rotational symmetry	Translation
Vector	Initial point
Terminal point	Component form
Glide reflection	Composition
Frieze pattern	

Review your notes and Chapter 7 by using the Chapter Review on pages 446–448 of your textbook.

8.1 Ratio and Proportion

Goals • Find and simplify the ratio of two numbers.
• Use proportions to solve real-life problems.

VOCABULARY

Ratio of *a* to *b*

Proportion

Extremes

Means

Example 1 *Simplifying Ratios*

Simplify the ratio.

a. $\dfrac{16 \text{ kg}}{800 \text{ g}}$

b. $\dfrac{7 \text{ ft}}{21 \text{ yd}}$

Solution

To simplify ratios with unlike units, convert to like units so that the units divide out. Then simplify the fraction, if possible.

a. $\dfrac{16 \text{ kg}}{800 \text{ g}} = \dfrac{16 \cdot \boxed{} \text{ g}}{800 \text{ g}} = \dfrac{\boxed{}}{800} = \underline{}$

b. $\dfrac{7 \text{ ft}}{21 \text{ yd}} = \underline{} = \underline{} = \underline{}$

Example 2 *Using Ratios*

The perimeter of rectangle *JKLM* is 56 centimeters. The ratio of *JK* : *KL* is 4 : 3. Find the length and width of the rectangle.

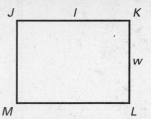

Solution

Because the ratio of *JK* : *KL* is ___ : ___ , you can represent the length of *JK* as ___ *x* and the width of $\overline{KL}$ as ___ *x*.

$2l + 2w = P$	Formula for perimeter of rectangle
$2(\underline{}x) + 2(\underline{}x) = 56$	Substitute for *l*, *w*, and *P*.
$\underline{}x + \underline{}x = 56$	Multiply.
$\underline{}x = 56$	Combine like terms.
$x = \underline{}$	Divide each side by ___ .

Answer So, *JKLM* has a length of ____ centimeters and a width of ____ centimeters.

✓ *Checkpoint* Simplify the ratio.

1. $\dfrac{5 \text{ km}}{200 \text{ m}}$	2. $\dfrac{40 \text{ oz}}{5 \text{ lb}}$

PROPERTIES OF PROPORTIONS

1. **Cross Product Property** The product of the extremes equals the product of the means.

   If $\dfrac{a}{b} = \dfrac{c}{d}$, then ____ = ____ .

2. **Reciprocal Property** If two ratios are equal, then their reciprocals are also equal.

   If $\dfrac{a}{b} = \dfrac{c}{d}$, then $\dfrac{}{} = \dfrac{}{}$.

Example 3 Solving Proportions

Solve the proportion $\dfrac{t+4}{8} = \dfrac{t}{3}$.

$\dfrac{t+4}{8} = \dfrac{t}{3}$ Write original proportion.

$\underline{\quad}(t+4) = \underline{\quad}t$ Cross product property

$\underline{\quad}t + \underline{\quad} = \underline{\quad}t$ Distributive property

$\underline{\quad} = t$ Simplify.

Example 4 Solving a Proportion

A scale model of a car is 10 inches long and 5 inches tall. The actual car is 60 inches tall. What is the length of the actual car?

Verbal Model $\dfrac{\text{Length of car}}{\text{Length of model}} = \dfrac{\text{Height of car}}{\text{Height of model}}$

Labels   Length of car $= x$ Height of car $= \underline{\quad}$ (in.)

Length of model $= \underline{\quad}$ Height of model $= \underline{\quad}$ (in.)

Reasoning $\dfrac{\quad}{\quad} = \dfrac{\quad}{\quad}$ Substitute.

$x = \dfrac{\quad}{\quad}$ Multiply each side by $\underline{\quad}$.

$x = \underline{\quad}$ Simplify.

Answer So, the actual car is $\underline{\quad}$ inches, or $\underline{\quad}$ feet long.

✔ **Checkpoint** Solve the proportion.

3. $\dfrac{7}{2} = \dfrac{21}{r}$	4. $\dfrac{6}{3x-12} = \dfrac{4}{x}$

Problem Solving in Geometry with Proportions

Goals • Use properties of proportions.
• Use proportions to solve real-life problems.

VOCABULARY

Geometric mean

ADDITIONAL PROPERTIES OF PROPORTIONS

3. If $\dfrac{a}{b} = \underline{}$, then $\dfrac{a}{c} = \underline{}$.

4. If $\dfrac{a}{b} = \underline{}$, then $\dfrac{a+b}{b} = \dfrac{\boxed{} + \boxed{}}{\boxed{}}$.

Example 1   *Using Properties of Proportions*

Tell whether the statement is true.

If $\dfrac{v}{5} = \dfrac{w}{9}$, then $\dfrac{v+5}{5} = \dfrac{w+5}{9}$.

Solution

$\dfrac{v}{5} = \dfrac{w}{9}$ **Given**

$\dfrac{v + \boxed{}}{5} = \dfrac{w + \boxed{}}{9}$ If $\dfrac{a}{b} = \dfrac{c}{d}$, then $\dfrac{a + \boxed{}}{b} = \dfrac{c + \boxed{}}{d}$.

Because $\dfrac{w + \boxed{}}{9} \underline{} \dfrac{w+5}{9}$, the conclusions are

$\underline{}$.

Answer The statement is $\underline{}$.

Example 2   *Using Properties of Proportions*

In the diagram $\dfrac{HJ}{JL} = \dfrac{GK}{KL}$. Find the length of $\overline{GK}$.

Solution

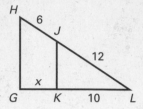

$\dfrac{HJ}{JL} = \dfrac{GK}{KL}$ **Given.**

$\underline{\hspace{1.5em}} = \dfrac{x}{\boxed{}}$ **Substitute.**

$\underline{\hspace{1em}}\, x = \underline{\hspace{1em}}$ **Cross product property**

$x = \underline{\hspace{1em}}$ **Divide each side by __.**

Answer So, the length of $\overline{GK}$ is __.

Example 3   *Using a Geometric Mean*

The two buildings shown have the same width-to-length ratio. The distance labeled x is the geometric mean of 105 m and 210 m. Find the value of x.

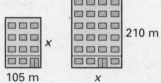

Solution

$\dfrac{\boxed{}}{x} = \dfrac{x}{\boxed{}}$ **Write proportion.**

$x^2 = \underline{\hspace{2em}} \cdot \underline{\hspace{2em}}$ **Cross product property**

$x = \underline{\hspace{3em}}$ **Simplify.**

$x = \underline{\hspace{3em}}$ **Factor.**

$x = \underline{\hspace{2em}}\sqrt{2}$ **Simplify.**

Answer The geometric mean of 105 and 210 is $\underline{\hspace{2em}}\sqrt{2}$, or about $\underline{\hspace{2em}}$. So, the distance labeled x in the diagram is about $\underline{\hspace{2em}}$ m.

1. Tell whether the statement is true: If $\frac{m}{7} = \frac{n}{11}$, then $\frac{m}{n} = \frac{7}{11}$.

---

2. In the diagram, $\frac{ST}{TV} = \frac{WX}{VW}$. Find ST.

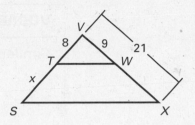

---

3. Find the geometric mean of 54 and 192.

Example 4   *Solving a Proportion*

You have a 10-by-8 inch photo of the school band that must be reduced to a length of 5.5 inches for the school yearbook. What is the width of the reduced photo?

8 in.

10 in.

5.5 in.

x

Solution

Verbal Model	$\dfrac{\text{Length of original}}{\text{Length of reduced}} = \dfrac{\text{Width of original}}{\text{Width of reduced}}$

Labels   Length of original photo = ___   (inches)

Length of reduced photo = ____   (inches)

Width of original photo = __   (inches)

Width of reduced photo = x   (inches)

Reasoning $\underline{\quad} = \dfrac{\square}{x}$ **Substitute.**

___ x = __ (____)   **Cross product property**

x = ____   **Use a calculator.**

Answer So, the reduced photo has a width of ____ inches.

8.3 Similar Polygons

Goals • Identify similar polygons.
• Use similar polygons to solve real-life problems.

VOCABULARY

Similar polygons

Scale factor

Example 1   *Comparing Similar Polygons*

Decide whether the figures are similar. If they are similar, write a similarity statement.

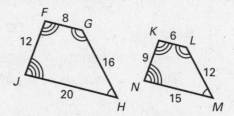

Solution

As shown, the corresponding angles of *FGHJ* and *KLMN* are congruent. Also, the corresponding side lengths are proportional.

$$\frac{FG}{KL} = \underline{\quad} = \underline{\quad} \qquad \frac{GH}{LM} = \underline{\quad} = \underline{\quad}$$

$$\frac{HJ}{MN} = \underline{\quad} = \underline{\quad} \qquad \frac{FJ}{KN} = \underline{\quad} = \underline{\quad}$$

Answer So, the two figures are similar and you can write

_____ ~ _____.

✔ Checkpoint Decide whether the figures are similar. If they are, write the similarity statement.

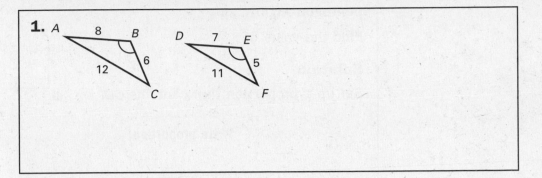

1.

Example 2 Comparing Photographic Enlargements

You have a 4-inch by 6-inch photo that you want to use for class election posters. You want the enlargement to be 26 inches wide. How long will it be?

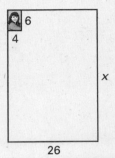

Solution

Compare the enlargement to the original measurements of the photo.

$$\frac{26 \text{ in.}}{4 \text{ in.}} = \frac{x \text{ In.}}{6 \text{ in.}}$$

$$x = \underline{\quad} \cdot \underline{\quad}$$

$$x = \underline{\quad} \text{ inches}$$

Answer The length of the enlargement will be ___ inches.

THEOREM 8.1

If two polygons are similar, then the ratio of their perimeters is equal to the ratios of their corresponding side lengths.

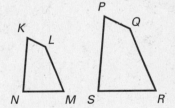

If *KLMN* ~ *PQRS*, then

$$\frac{KL + LM + MN + NK}{PQ + QR + RS + SP} = \underline{\quad} = \underline{\quad} = \underline{\quad} = \underline{\quad} \, .$$

Example 3   *Using Similar Polygons*

Pentagon *CDFGH* is similar to
pentagon *JKLMN*.

Find the value of *x*.

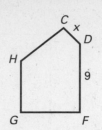

Solution

Set up a proportion that contains *CD*.

$$\frac{CD}{DF} = \underline{\quad\quad}$$ **Write proportion.**

$$\frac{x}{\boxed{}} = \underline{\quad\quad}$$ **Substitute.**

$$x = \underline{\quad}$$ **Cross multiply and divide by __.**

✔ *Checkpoint* **Complete the following exercises.**

2. Verify that these two triangles
   are similar. Write the similarity
   statement. Then find the ratio
   of their perimeters.

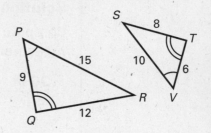

3. Parallelogram *JKLM* is
   similar to parallelogram
   PQRS. Find the value
   of *x*.

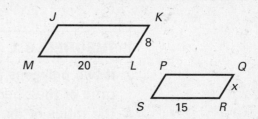

8.4 Similar Triangles

Goals • Identify similar triangles.
• Use similar triangles in real-life problems.

Example 1   *Writing Proportionality Statements*

In the diagram, $\triangle GST \sim \triangle GNP$.

a. Write the statement of proportionality.

b. Find $m\angle GNP$.

c. Find GP.

Solution

a. $\dfrac{GN}{\boxed{}} = \dfrac{GP}{\boxed{}} = \dfrac{NP}{\boxed{}}$

b. $\angle NST \cong \angle GNP$, so $m\angle GNP = \underline{\quad}°$.

c.

$\dfrac{NP}{\boxed{}} = \dfrac{GP}{\boxed{}}$ **Write proportion.**

$\dfrac{15}{\boxed{}} = \dfrac{GP}{\boxed{}}$ **Substitute.**

$\dfrac{\boxed{}(15)}{\boxed{}} = GP$ **Multiply each side by ____.**

$\underline{\quad\quad} = GP$ **Simplify.**

Answer So, GP is _____ units.

POSTULATE 25: ANGLE-ANGLE (AA) SIMILARITY POSTULATE

If two angles of one triangle are
congruent to two angles of another
triangle, then the two triangles
are similar.

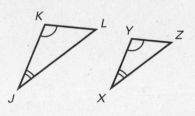

If $\angle JKL \cong \angle XYZ$ and $\angle KJL \cong \angle YXZ$,
then $\triangle \underline{\quad\quad} \sim \triangle \underline{\quad\quad}$.

Example 2　*Proving that Two Triangles are Similar*

In the diagram, $\triangle ABH \sim \triangle KLH$. Use properties of similar triangles to explain why these triangles are similar.

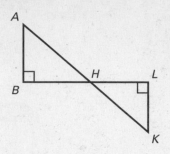

Solution

You can use the Vertical Angles Theorem to determine $\angle AHB \cong \angle$_____. Because they are right angles, $\angle ABH \cong \angle$_____.
By the _____, you can conclude that $\triangle ABH \sim \triangle KLH$.

Example 3　*Using Similar Triangles*

To comply with the Americans with Disabilities Act, wheelchair ramps made for new constructions must have a height to length ratio of $1:12$. At a new construction, the height h to the bottom of a door is 2.5 feet. Use the proportion $\dfrac{a}{b} = \dfrac{h}{r}$ to estimate the length r that the ramp should be to have the correct slope ratio. In the proportion, use $a = 1$ ft and $b = 12$ ft.

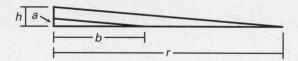

Solution

$$\frac{a}{b} = \frac{h}{r} \qquad \textbf{Write proportion.}$$

$$\frac{\boxed{}}{\boxed{}} = \frac{\boxed{}}{r} \qquad \textbf{Substitute.}$$

$$r = \underline{\quad} \text{ ft} \qquad \textbf{Cross product property}$$

Answer The ramp should have a length of ____ feet.

Example 4 **Using Scale Factors**

Find the length of $\overline{MS}$.

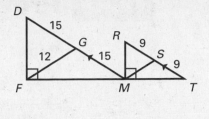

First, find the scale factor of
$\triangle DFM$ to $\triangle RMT$.

$$\frac{DM}{RT} = \frac{\boxed{} + \boxed{}}{\boxed{} + \boxed{}} = \frac{\boxed{}}{\boxed{}} = \underline{}$$

Now, because the ratio of the lengths of the segments is equal to
the scale factor, you can write the following equation.

$$\frac{FG}{MS} = \underline{}$$

Answer Substitute ___ for *FG* and solve for *MS* to show that
$MS = \underline{}$.

✔ *Checkpoint* **Complete the following exercises.**

1. You are standing 15 m from building A and 50 m from building B. Building A is 90 m tall. Find the height of building B. 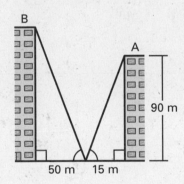	**2.** $\triangle JNL \sim \triangle RTS$. Find the length of $\overline{KN}$. 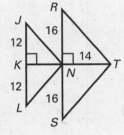

8.5 Proving Triangles are Similar

Goals • Use similarity theorems to prove two triangles are similar.
• Use similar triangles to solve real-life problems.

THEOREM 8.2: SIDE-SIDE-SIDE (SSS) SIMILARITY THEOREM

If the lengths of the corresponding sides of two triangles are proportional, then the triangles are similar.

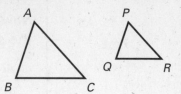

If $\dfrac{AB}{PQ} = \dfrac{BC}{QR} = \dfrac{CA}{RP}$,

then $\triangle$_____ $\sim$ $\triangle$_____.

THEOREM 8.3: SIDE-ANGLE-SIDE (SAS) SIMILARITY THEOREM

If an angle of one triangle is congruent to an angle of a second triangle and the lengths of the sides including these angles are proportional, then the triangles are similar.

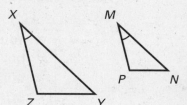

If $\angle X \cong \angle M$ and $\dfrac{ZX}{PM} = \dfrac{XY}{MN}$,

then $\triangle$_____ $\sim$ $\triangle$_____.

Example 1 *Using the SSS Similarity Theorem*

Which of the following three triangles are similar?

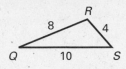 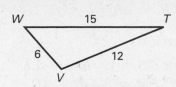 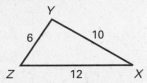

To decide which, if any, of the triangles are similar, you need to consider the ratios of the lengths of corresponding sides.

Ratios of Side Lengths of △QRS and △TVW

Shortest sides	Longest sides	Remaining sides
$\dfrac{RS}{VW} = \underline{\quad} = \underline{\quad}$,	$\dfrac{QS}{TW} = \underline{\quad} = \underline{\quad}$,	$\dfrac{QR}{TV} = \underline{\quad} = \underline{\quad}$

Answer Because the ratios are equal, _____.

Ratios of Side Lengths of △QRS and △XYZ

Shortest sides	Longest sides	Remaining sides
$\dfrac{RS}{YZ} = \underline{\quad} = \underline{\quad}$,	$\dfrac{QS}{XZ} = \underline{\quad} = \underline{\quad}$,	$\dfrac{QR}{XY} = \underline{\quad} = \underline{\quad}$

Answer Because the ratios are not equal, _____

_____.

✔ *Checkpoint* **Complete the following exercise.**

1. Which of the three triangles are similar?

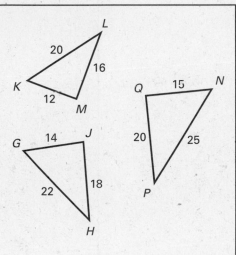

Example 2 *Using the SAS Similarity Theorem*

Use the given lengths to prove that
$\triangle DFR \sim \triangle MNR$.

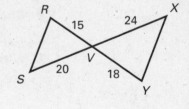

Solution

Given: $DF = 15$, $MN = 12$
    $DM = 2$, $DR = 10$

Prove: $\triangle DFR \sim \triangle MNR$

Paragraph Proof Use the SAS Similarity
Theorem. Begin by finding the ratios of the
lengths of the corresponding sides.

$$\frac{DF}{MN} = \underline{\qquad} = \underline{\qquad}$$

$$\frac{DR}{MR} = \underline{\qquad} = \underline{\qquad} = \underline{\qquad}$$

So, the lengths of sides $\overline{DF}$ and $\overline{DR}$ are _____ to the
lengths of the corresponding sides of $\triangle MNR$. Because $\angle FDR$ and
$\angle NMR$ are _____, use the _____ Theorem to
conclude that $\triangle DFR \sim \triangle MNR$.

✓ *Checkpoint* Complete the following exercise.

2. Describe how to prove that $\triangle RSV$ is
similar to $\triangle YXV$.

8.6 Proportions and Similar Triangles

Goals • Use proportionality theorems to calculate segment lengths.
• Solve real-life problems.

THEOREM 8.4: TRIANGLE PROPORTIONALITY THEOREM

If a line parallel to one side of a triangle intersects the other two sides, then it divides the two sides _____.

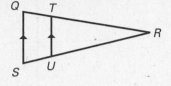

If $\overline{TU} \parallel \overline{QS}$, then $\dfrac{}{} = \dfrac{}{}$.

THEOREM 8.5: CONVERSE OF THE TRIANGLE PROPORTIONALITY THEOREM

If a line divides two sides of a triangle proportionally, then it is parallel to the

_____.

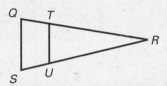

If $\dfrac{RT}{TQ} = \dfrac{RU}{US}$, then ____ $\parallel$ ____.

Example 1   *Finding the Length of a Segment*

What is the length of $\overline{NR}$?

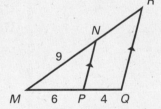

Solution

$\dfrac{PQ}{MP} = \dfrac{NR}{MN}$ Theorem ____

$\dfrac{\square}{\square} = \dfrac{NR}{\square}$ Substitute.

$\underline{} = NR$ Multiply each side by ___.

$\underline{} = NR$ Simplify.

Answer So, the length of $\overline{NR}$ is ___.

1. Find the length of $\overline{DF}$.

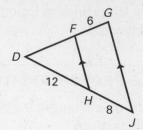

2. Given the diagram, determine whether $\overline{MN}$ is parallel to $\overline{PQ}$.

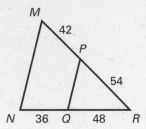

THEOREM 8.6

If three parallel lines intersect two transversals, then they divide the transversals _____.

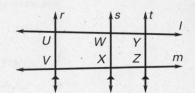

   If $r \parallel s$ and $s \parallel t$, and ℓ and m

   intersect r, s, and t, then ____ = ____ .

THEOREM 8.7

If a ray bisects an angle of a triangle, then it divides the opposite side into segments whose lengths are _____ to the lengths of the other two sides.

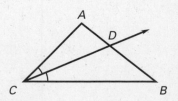

   If $\overrightarrow{CD}$ bisects $\angle ACB$, then ____ = ____ .

Example 2 | *Using Proportionality Theorems*

What is the length of $\overline{GH}$?

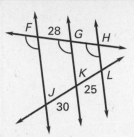

Solution

Because corresponding angles are congruent, the lines are parallel and you can use Theorem 8.6.

$$\frac{FG}{GH} = \frac{JK}{KL} \qquad \text{Parallel lines divide transversals proportionally.}$$

$$\frac{\boxed{}}{GH} = \frac{}{\underline{}} \qquad \text{Substitute.}$$

$$\underline{} \cdot \underline{} = \underline{} \cdot GH \qquad \text{Cross product property.}$$

$$\frac{}{\underline{}} = GH \qquad \text{Divide each side by } \underline{} \text{ and simplify.}$$

Answer So, the length of $\overline{GH}$ is $\underline{}$, or $\underline{}$.

Example 3 | *Using Proportionality Theorems*

In the diagram, $\angle QPR \cong \angle RPS$. Use the given side lengths to find the length of $\overline{QR}$.

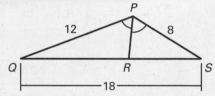

Solution

Because $\overline{PR}$ is an angle bisector of $\angle QPS$, you can apply Theorem 8.7.

Let $x = QR$. Then, $RS = 18 - x$.

$$\frac{PS}{QP} = \frac{RS}{QR} \qquad \text{Apply Theorem 8.7.}$$

$$\frac{}{\underline{}} = \frac{\boxed{}}{x} \qquad \text{Substitute.}$$

$$\underline{} \cdot x = \underline{}(\underline{}) \qquad \text{Cross product property}$$

$$\underline{}x = \underline{} - \underline{}x \qquad \text{Distributive property}$$

$$\underline{}x = \underline{} \qquad \text{Add } \underline{} \text{ to each side.}$$

$$x = \underline{} \qquad \text{Divide each side by } \underline{}.$$

Answer So, the length of $\overline{QR}$ is $\underline{}$ units.

Example 4 **Finding the Length of a Segment**

Hiking Trails A state park has five trails, as shown in the diagram. The horizontal Red, Green, and Blue trails are evenly spaced. The River and Sky trails intersect the Red, Green and Blue trails. Explain why the distance between the Red and Green trails on the Sky trail is the same as the distance between the Green and Blue trails on the Sky trail.

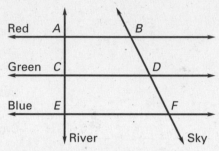

Solution

Because the Red, Green, and Blue trails are each _____, you know that they are parallel to each other. Using Theorem ____, you can conclude that $\frac{AC}{CE} = $ ____. Because the trails are evenly spaced, you know that $AC = CE$. So, you can conclude that ____ = ____, which means that the distance between the Red and Green trails and the Green and Blue trails on the Sky trail have the same lengths.

✔ **Checkpoint** Complete the following exercises.

---

3. In the diagram, $\overline{HK} \parallel \overline{LM} \parallel \overline{NP}$, $HL = 2.4$, $KM = 2.8$, and $MP = 4.9$. Find the length of $\overline{LN}$.

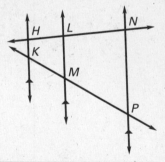

---

4. Find the value of x.

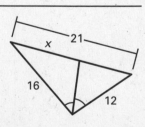

8.7 Dilations

Goals • Identify dilations.
• Use properties of dilations in real-life.

VOCABULARY

Dilation

Enlargement

Reduction

Example 1   *Identifying Dilations*

Identify the dilation and find its scale factor.

a.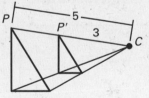
b.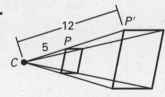

Solution

a. Because $\dfrac{CP'}{CP} =$ _____ , the scale factor is $k =$ _____ . This is

   a _____ .

b. Because $\dfrac{CP'}{CP} =$ _____ , the scale factor is $k =$ _____ . This is

   an _____ .

Example 2 *Dilation in a Coordinate Plane*

Draw a dilation of △XYZ. Use the origin as the center and use a scale factor of 2. Find the perimeter of the preimage and the perimeter of the image.

Solution

Because the center of the dilation is the origin, you can find the image of each vertex by multiplying its coordinates by the _____.

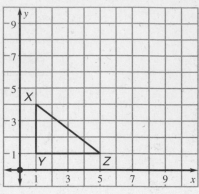

$X(1, 4) \rightarrow X'(\underline{\hspace{0.5cm}}, \underline{\hspace{0.5cm}})$

$Y(1, 1) \rightarrow Y'(\underline{\hspace{0.5cm}}, \underline{\hspace{0.5cm}})$

$Z(5, 1) \rightarrow Z'(\underline{\hspace{0.5cm}}, \underline{\hspace{0.5cm}})$

To find the perimeters of the preimage and image, you need to find XZ and $X'Z'$.

$$XZ = \sqrt{(\underline{\hspace{0.3cm}} - \underline{\hspace{0.3cm}})^2 + (\underline{\hspace{0.3cm}} - \underline{\hspace{0.3cm}})^2} = \sqrt{(\underline{\hspace{0.5cm}})^2 + \underline{\hspace{0.3cm}}^2}$$
$$= \sqrt{\underline{\hspace{0.3cm}} + \underline{\hspace{0.3cm}}} = \sqrt{\underline{\hspace{0.5cm}}} = \underline{\hspace{0.3cm}}$$

Perimeter of △XYZ = ___ + ___ + ___ = ___

$$X'Z' = \sqrt{(\underline{\hspace{0.3cm}} - \underline{\hspace{0.3cm}})^2 + (\underline{\hspace{0.3cm}} - \underline{\hspace{0.3cm}})^2} = \sqrt{(\underline{\hspace{0.5cm}})^2 + \underline{\hspace{0.3cm}}^2}$$
$$= \sqrt{\underline{\hspace{0.3cm}} + \underline{\hspace{0.3cm}}} = \sqrt{\underline{\hspace{0.5cm}}} = \underline{\hspace{0.3cm}}$$

Perimeter of △X'Y'Z' = ___ + ___ + ___ = ___

✓ *Checkpoint* **Use the dilation shown.**

1. Is the dilation shown a reduction or an enlargement?

2. What is the scale factor?

3. What are the coordinates of the vertices of the image?

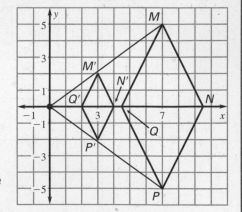

Words to Review

Give an example of the vocabulary word.

Ratio	Proportion
Extremes	**Means**
Geometric mean	**Similar polygons**
Scale factor	**Dilation**

Reduction	Enlargement

Review your notes and Chapter 8 by using the Chapter Review on pages 516–518 of your textbook.

9.1 Similar Right Triangles

Goals • Solve problems involving similar right triangles formed by the altitude drawn to the hypotenuse of a right triangle.
• Use a geometric mean to solve problems.

THEOREM 9.1

If the altitude is drawn to the hypotenuse of a right triangle, then the two triangles formed are _____ to the original triangle and to each other.

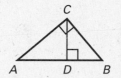

$\triangle CBD \sim \triangle ABC$, $\triangle ACD \sim \triangle ABC$, and $\triangle CBD \sim \triangle ACD$

Example 1 *Finding the Height of a Ramp*

Ramp Height A ramp has a cross section that is a right triangle. The diagram shows the approximate dimensions of this cross section. Find the height h of the ramp.

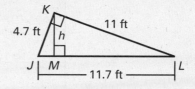

Solution

By Theorem 9.1, $\triangle$_____ $\sim \triangle$_____.

Use similar triangles to write a proportion.

$$\frac{KM}{\boxed{}} = \frac{}{}$$ Corresponding side lengths are in proportion.

$$\frac{h}{\boxed{}} = \frac{}{}$$ Substitute.

$$\underline{}\,h = \underline{}(\underline{})$$ Cross product property

$$h \approx \underline{}$$ Solve for h.

Answer The height of the ramp is about _____ feet.

Checkpoint Write similarity statements for the three triangles in the diagram. Then find the given length. Round decimals to the nearest tenth, if necessary.

1. Find *AD*.

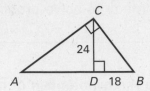

2. Find *NQ*.

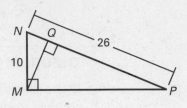

GEOMETRIC MEAN THEOREMS

THEOREM 9.2

In a right triangle, the altitude from the right angle to the hypotenuse divides the hypotenuse into two segments.

The length of the altitude is the _____ of the lengths of the two segments.

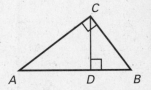

$$\frac{BD}{\boxed{}} = \frac{\boxed{}}{AD}$$

THEOREM 9.3

In a right triangle, the altitude from the right angle to the hypotenuse divides the hypotenuse into two segments.

The length of each leg of the right triangle is the geometric mean of the lengths of the hypotenuse and the segment of the hypotenuse that is _____ to the leg.

$$\frac{AB}{CB} = \frac{CB}{\boxed{}}$$

$$\frac{AB}{AC} = \frac{AC}{\boxed{}}$$

Example 2 *Using a Geometric Mean*

Find the value of each variable.

a.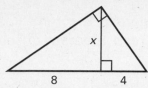

b.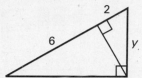

Solution

a. Apply Theorem 9.2.

$$\frac{\boxed{}}{x} = \underline{}$$

$$\underline{} = \underline{}$$

$$\underline{} = x$$

$$\underline{} = x$$

b. Apply Theorem 9.3.

$$\underline{} = \frac{y}{\boxed{}}$$

$$\underline{} = \frac{y}{\boxed{}}$$

$$\underline{} = \underline{}$$

$$\underline{} = y$$

✔ **Checkpoint** Find the value of the variable.

3.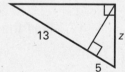

4.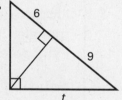

5.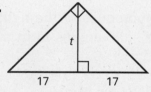

9.2 The Pythagorean Theorem

Goals • Prove the Pythagorean Theorem.
• Use the Pythagorean Theorem to solve problems.

VOCABULARY

Pythagorean triple

THEOREM 9.4: PYTHAGOREAN THEOREM

In a right triangle, the _____ of the length
of the hypotenuse is equal to the sum of the
_____ of the lengths of the legs.

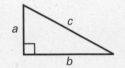

$$c^2 = a^2 + b^2$$

Example 1 *Finding the Length of a Hypotenuse*

Find the length of the hypotenuse of the right
triangle. Tell whether the side lengths form a
Pythagorean triple.

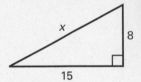

Solution

$(\text{hypotenuse})^2 = (\text{leg})^2 + (\text{leg})^2$	Pythagorean Theorem
$x^2 = \underline{}^2 + \underline{}^2$	Substitute.
$x^2 = \underline{} + \underline{}$	Multiply.
$x^2 = \underline{}$	Add.
$x = \underline{}$	Find the positive square root.

Answer The length of the hypotenuse is ___. Because the
side lengths 8, 15, and ___ are _____, they form a
Pythagorean triple.

Example 2 *Finding the Length of a Leg*

Find the length of the leg of the right triangle.

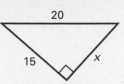

Solution

$$(\text{hypotenuse})^2 = (\text{leg})^2 + (\text{leg})^2 \qquad \text{Pythagorean Theorem}$$

$$\underline{\quad}^2 = x^2 + \underline{\quad}^2 \qquad \text{Substitute.}$$

$$\underline{\quad\quad} = x^2 + \underline{\quad\quad} \qquad \text{Multiply.}$$

$$\underline{\quad\quad} = x^2 \qquad \text{Subtract} \underline{\quad\quad} \text{ from each side.}$$

$$\sqrt{\underline{\quad\quad}} = x \qquad \text{Find the positive square root.}$$

$$\sqrt{\underline{\quad}} \cdot \sqrt{\underline{\quad}} = x \qquad \text{Use product property.}$$

$$\underline{\quad\quad} = x \qquad \text{Simplify the radical.}$$

Answer The length of the leg is _____ .

✔ *Checkpoint* Find the value of x. Simplify answers that are radicals. Then tell whether the side lengths form a Pythagorean triple.

1. 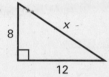	**2.** 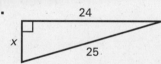

Example 3 *Finding the Area of a Triangle*

Find the area of the triangle to the
nearest tenth of a square inch.

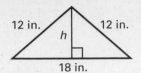

Solution

You are given that the base of the
triangle is ___ inches, but you do not know the
height *h*.

Because the triangle is isosceles, it can be divided
into two congruent right angles with the given
dimensions. Use the Pythagorean Theorem to find
the value of *h*.

$$\underline{}^2 = \underline{}^2 + h^2 \qquad \text{Pythagorean Theorem}$$

$$\underline{} = \underline{} + h^2 \qquad \text{Multiply.}$$

$$\underline{} = h^2 \qquad \text{Subtract } \underline{} \text{ from each side.}$$

$$\sqrt{\underline{}} = h \qquad \text{Find the positive square root.}$$

$$\underline{} = h \qquad \text{Simplify the radical.}$$

Now find the area of the original triangle.

$$A = \frac{1}{2}bh \qquad \text{Area of a triangle}$$

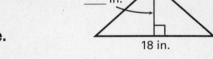

$$= \frac{1}{2}(\underline{})(\underline{}) \qquad \text{Substitute.}$$

$$\approx \underline{} \qquad \text{Use a calculator.}$$

Answer The area of the triangle is about _____ square inches.

✔ Checkpoint Find the area of the triangle. Round your answer
to the nearest tenth.

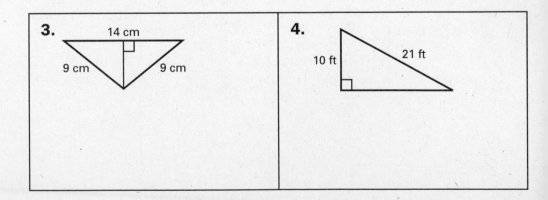

3. 14 cm

9 cm   9 cm

4.

10 ft   21 ft

9.3 The Converse of the Pythagorean Theorem

Goals • Use the Converse of the Pythagorean Theorem to solve problems.
• Use side lengths to classify triangles by their angle measures.

THEOREM 9.5: CONVERSE OF THE PYTHAGOREAN THEOREM

If the square of the length of the longest side of a triangle is equal to the sum of the squares of the lengths of the other two sides, then the triangle is a _____ triangle.

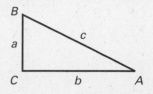

If $c^2 = a^2 + b^2$, then $\triangle ABC$ is a _____ triangle.

Example 1 *Verifying Right Triangles*

Tell whether the triangle at the right is a right triangle.

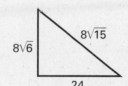

Solution

Let c represent the length of the longest side of the triangle. Check to see whether the side lengths satisfy the equation $c^2 = a^2 + b^2$.

$$(\underline{\quad\quad})^2 \overset{?}{=} (\underline{\quad\quad})^2 + \underline{\quad}^2$$

$$\underline{\quad}^2 \cdot (\underline{\quad\quad})^2 \overset{?}{=} \underline{\quad}^2 \cdot (\underline{\quad\quad})^2 + \underline{\quad}^2$$

$$\underline{\quad} \cdot \underline{\quad} \overset{?}{=} \underline{\quad} \cdot \underline{\quad} + \underline{\quad}$$

$$\underline{\quad\quad} \overset{?}{=} \underline{\quad\quad} + \underline{\quad\quad}$$

$$\underline{\quad\quad} = \underline{\quad\quad}$$

Answer The triangle _____ a right triangle.

1.

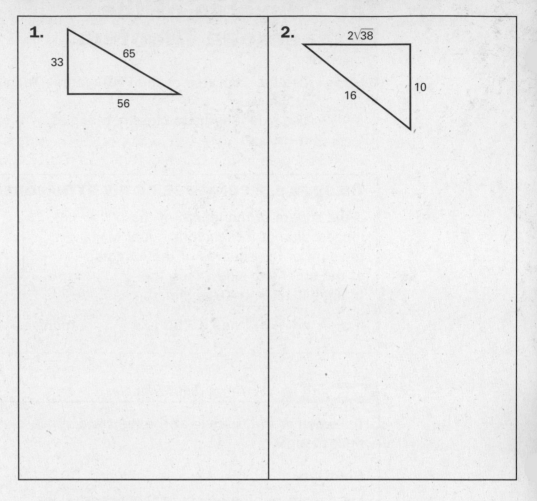

33   65

56

2.

$2\sqrt{38}$

16   10

THEOREM 9.6

If the square of the length of the longest side of a triangle is less than the sum of the squares of the lengths of the other two sides, then the triangle is _____.

   If $c^2 < a^2 + b^2$, then $\triangle ABC$ is _____.

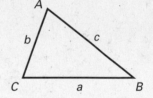

THEOREM 9.7

If the square of the length of the longest side of a triangle is greater than the sum of the squares of the lengths of the other two sides, then the triangle is _____.

   If $c^2 > a^2 + b^2$, then $\triangle ABC$ is _____.

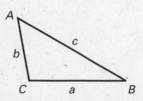

Example 2 *Classifying Triangles*

Decide whether the set of numbers can represent the side lengths of a triangle. If they can, classify the triangle as *right*, *acute*, or *obtuse*.

a. 28, 40, 48   **b. 5.7, 12.2, 13.9**

Solution

Compare the square of the length of the longest side with the sum of the squares of the lengths of the two shorter sides.

a. c^2 _?_ $a^2 + b^2$ Compare c^2 with $a^2 + b^2$.

   ____^{2} _?_ $28^2 +$ ____^{2} Substitute.

   _____ _?_ ____ $+$ _____   Multiply.

   _____ __ _____ c^2 is ____ than $a^2 + b^2$.

   Answer Because c^2 ___ $a^2 + b^2$, the triangle is _____.

b. c^2 _?_ $a^2 + b^2$ Compare c^2 with $a^2 + b^2$.

   ____^{2} _?_ ____$^2 + 12.2^2$ Substitute.

   _____ _?_ _____ $+$ _____   Multiply.

   _____ __ _____ c^2 is _____ than $a^2 + b^2$.

   Answer Because c^2 ___ $a^2 + b^2$, the triangle is _____.

✔ *Checkpoint* Can the numbers represent the side lengths of a triangle? If so, classify the triangle as *right*, *acute*, or *obtuse*.

3. 16, 30, 34	**4.** 8, 13, 22	**5.** 6, 9, 12

9.4 Special Right Triangles

Goals • Find the side lengths of special right triangles.
• Use special right triangles to solve real-life problems.

VOCABULARY

Special right triangles

THEOREM 9.8: 45°-45°-90° TRIANGLE THEOREM

In a 45°-45°-90° triangle, the hypotenuse
is _____ times as long as each leg.

    Hypotenuse = _____ • leg

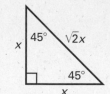

THEOREM 9.9: 30°-60°-90° TRIANGLE THEOREM

In a 30°-60°-90° triangle, the hypotenuse is
twice as long as the _____ leg, and the
longer leg is _____ times as long as the
shorter leg.

    Hypotenuse = 2 • _____ leg

    Longer leg = _____ • shorter leg

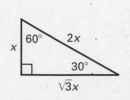

Example 1 — Finding the Hypotenuse in a 45°-45°-90° Triangle

Find the value of x.

By the Triangle Sum Theorem, the measure of the third angle is ____°. The triangle is a ____°-____°-90° right triangle, so the length x of the hypotenuse is _____ times the length of a leg.

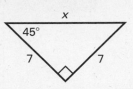

Hypotenuse = _____ • leg   ____°-____°-90° Triangle Theorem

x = _____ • ___   Substitute.

x = _____   Simplify.

Example 2 — Side Lengths in a 30°-60°-90° Triangle

Find the values of s and t.

Because the triangle is a 30°-60°-90° triangle, the longer leg is _____ times the length of the shorter leg.

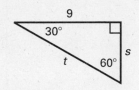

Longer leg = _____ • shorter leg   30°-60°-90° Triangle Theorem

__ = _____ • s   Substitute.

_____ = s   Divide each side by _____.

_____ • _____ = s   Multiply numerator and denominator by _____.

_____ = s   Simplify.

The length of the hypotenuse is _____ the length of the shorter leg.

Hypotenuse = __ • shorter leg   30°-60°-90° Triangle Theorem

t = __ • _____   Substitute.

t = _____   Simplify.

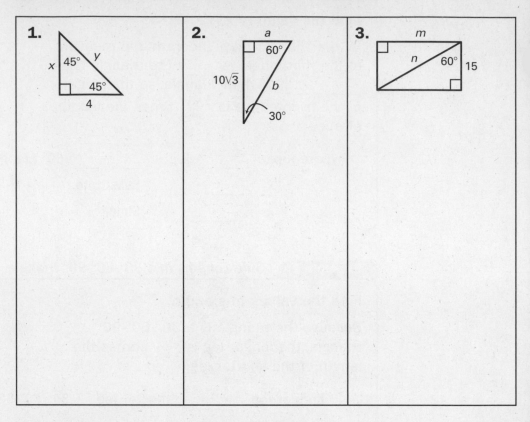

✔ **Checkpoint** Find the values of the variables.

1. 45° y / x 45° / 4

2. a / 60° / 10√3 / b / 30°

3. m / n 60° 15

Example 3 **Finding the Area of a Window**

Construction The window is a square. Find the area of the window.

— 36√2 in.

Solution

First find the side length *s* of the window by dividing it into two ____°-____°-90° triangles. The length of the hypotenuse is _____ inches. Use this length to find *s*.

_____ = ____ • *s*   ____°-____°-90° Triangle Theorem

____ = *s*   Divide each side by ____.

Use *s* = ____ to find the area of the window.

$A = s^2$ **Area of a square**

$= \underline{}^2$ **Substitute.**

$= \underline{}$ **Multiply.**

Answer The area of the window is _____ square inches.

9.5 Trigonometric Ratios

Goals • Find the sine, the cosine, and the tangent of an acute angle.
• Use trigonometric ratios to solve real-life problems.

VOCABULARY

Trigonometric ratio

Sine

Cosine

Tangent

Angle of elevation

TRIGONOMETRIC RATIOS

Let $\triangle ABC$ be a right triangle. The sine, the cosine, and the tangent of acute $\angle A$ are defined as follows.

$\sin A = \dfrac{\text{side opposite } \angle A}{\text{hypotenuse}} = \underline{\hspace{1cm}}$

$\cos A = \dfrac{\text{side adjacent to } \angle A}{\text{hypotenuse}} = \underline{\hspace{1cm}}$

$\tan A = \dfrac{\text{side opposite } \angle A}{\text{side adjacent to } \angle A} = \underline{\hspace{1cm}}$

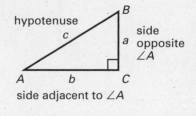

Example 1 **Finding Trigonometric Ratios**

Find the sine, the cosine, and the tangent
of ∠P.

Solution

The length of the hypotenuse is ____. The
length of the side opposite ∠P is ____, and the length of the side
adjacent to ∠P is ____.

sin P = _____ = ____ ≈ _____

cos P = _____ = ____ ≈ _____

tan P = _____ = ____ = _____

Example 2 **Trigonometric Ratios for 60°**

Find the sine, the cosine, and the tangent of 60°.

Solution

Begin by sketching a 30°-60°-90° triangle as
shown at the right. To make the calculations simple,
choose 1 as the length of the shorter leg. From the
30°-60°-90° Triangle Theorem, it follows that the
length of the longer leg is _____ and the length of the
hypotenuse is ____. Label these lengths in the diagram.

sin 60° = _____ = _____ ≈ _____

cos 60° = _____ = ____ = ____

tan 60° = _____ = ____ ≈ _____

✔ Checkpoint Use the diagram at the right to find the trigonometric ratio.

1. sin X

X ──12── Z

20   16

Y

_____

2. cos X

_____

3. tan Y

Example 3 *Indirect Measurement*

Flag Pole You are measuring the height of a flag pole. You stand 19 feet from the base of the pole. You measure the angle of elevation from a point on the ground to the top of the pole to be 64°. Estimate the height of the pole.

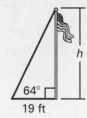

h

64°

19 ft

Solution

$$\underline{\qquad} = \frac{\text{opposite}}{\text{adjacent}}$$ **Write trigonometric ratio.**

$$\underline{\qquad} = \frac{\quad}{\underline{\quad}}$$ **Substitute.**

$$\underline{\qquad} = h$$ **Multiply each side by ___.**

$$\underline{\quad}(\underline{\qquad}) = h$$ **Evaluate tan 64°.**

$$\underline{\qquad} \approx h$$ **Simplify.**

Answer The height of the flag pole is about ____ feet.

9.6 Solving Right Triangles

Goals • Solve a right triangle.
• Use right triangles to solve real-life problems.

VOCABULARY

Solve a right triangle

Example 1   *Solving a Right Triangle*

Solve the right triangle. Round decimals to the nearest tenth.

Solution

Use the Pythagorean Theorem to find the length of the hypotenuse c.

$(\text{hypotenuse})^2 = (\text{leg})^2 + (\text{leg})^2$ **Pythagorean Theorem**

$c^2 = \underline{}^2 + \underline{}^2$ **Substitute.**

$c^2 = \underline{}$ **Simplify.**

$c = \underline{}$ **Find the positive square root.**

$c \approx \underline{}$ **Use a calculator to approximate.**

Use a calculator to find the measure of $\angle B$.

 (__ ÷ __) **2nd** **TAN** $\approx$ ____°

$\angle A$ and $\angle B$ are complementary. The sum of their measures is ____°.

$m\angle A + m\angle B = \underline{}°$ $\angle A$ and $\angle B$ are complementary.

$m\angle A + \underline{}° = \underline{}°$ **Substitute for $m\angle B$.**

$m\angle A = \underline{}°$ **Subtract.**

Answer The side lengths are __, __, and ____. The angle measures are ____°, ____°, and ___°.

Example 2 **Solving a Right Triangle**

Solve the right triangle. Round decimals to the nearest tenth.

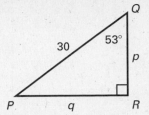

Solution

Use trigonometric ratios to find the values of p and q.

$$\sin Q = \frac{\text{opp.}}{\text{hyp.}} \qquad\qquad \cos Q = \frac{\text{adj.}}{\text{hyp.}}$$

$$\sin \underline{\quad}° = \frac{q}{\Box} \qquad\qquad \cos \underline{\quad}° = \frac{p}{\Box}$$

$$\underline{\quad} \sin \underline{\quad}° = q \qquad\qquad \underline{\quad} \cos \underline{\quad}° = p$$

$$\underline{\quad}(\underline{\qquad}) \approx q \qquad\qquad \underline{\quad}(\underline{\qquad}) \approx p$$

$$\underline{\qquad} \approx q \qquad\qquad \underline{\qquad} \approx p$$

$\angle P$ and $\angle Q$ are complementary. The sum of their measures is $\underline{\quad}°$.

$$m\angle P + m\angle Q = \underline{\quad}° \qquad \angle P \text{ and } \angle Q \text{ are complementary.}$$

$$m\angle P + \underline{\quad}° = \underline{\quad}° \qquad \text{Substitute for } m\angle Q.$$

$$m\angle P = \underline{\quad}° \qquad \text{Subtract.}$$

Answer The side lengths of the triangle are $\underline{\qquad}$, $\underline{\qquad}$, and $\underline{\quad}$. The angle measures are $\underline{\quad}°$, $\underline{\quad}°$, and $\underline{\quad}°$.

✔ **Checkpoint** Solve the right triangle. Round decimals to the nearest tenth.

1.

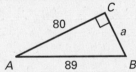

2.

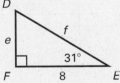

Example 3   *Solving a Right Triangle*

Sports When a hockey player is 35 feet from the goal line, he shoots the puck directly at the goal. The angle of elevation at which the puck leaves the ice is 7°. The height of the goal is 4 feet. Will the player score a goal?

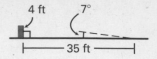

Solution

Begin by finding the height h of the puck at the goal line. Use a trigonometric ratio.

$$\tan \underline{\quad}° = \frac{\text{opp.}}{\text{adj.}} \qquad \text{Write trigonometric ratio.}$$

$$\tan \underline{\quad}° = \frac{h}{\boxed{}} \qquad \text{Substitute.}$$

$$\underline{\quad} \tan \underline{\quad}° = h \qquad \text{Multiply each side by } \underline{\quad}.$$

$$\underline{\quad}(\underline{\qquad}) \approx h \qquad \text{Use a calculator.}$$

$$\underline{\quad} \approx h \qquad \text{Multiply.}$$

Answer Because the height of the puck at the goal line (____ feet) is greater than the height of the goal (4 feet), the player _____ score a goal.

✓ *Checkpoint* **Complete the following exercise.**

3. A hockey player is 27 feet from the goal line. He shoots the puck directly at the goal. The height of the goal is 4 feet. What is the maximum angle of elevation at which the player can shoot the puck and still score a goal?

4 ft $x°$

|— 27 ft —|

9.7 Vectors

Goals • Find the magnitude and direction of a vector.
• Add vectors.

VOCABULARY

Magnitude of a vector

Direction of a vector

Equal vectors

Parallel vectors

Sum of vectors

Example 1   *Finding the Magnitude of a Vector*

$P(-4, 3)$ and $Q(2, -1)$ are the initial and terminal points of a vector. Draw $\overrightarrow{PQ}$ in a coordinate plane. Then find its magnitude.

Solution

Component form $= \langle x_2 - x_1, y_2 - y_1 \rangle$

$\overrightarrow{PQ} = \langle \underline{\ \ } - \underline{\ \ \ \ }, \underline{\ \ \ } - \underline{\ } \rangle$

$= \langle \underline{\ \ }, \underline{\ \ \ } \rangle$

Use the Distance Formula to find the magnitude.

$|\overrightarrow{PQ}| = \sqrt{[\underline{\ \ } - (\underline{\ \ \ })]^2 + (\underline{\ \ \ } - \underline{\ \ })^2} = \sqrt{\underline{\ \ \ }} \approx \underline{\ \ \ }$

Example 2 *Describing the Direction of a Vector*

The vector $\overrightarrow{CD}$ describes the velocity of a moving hot air balloon. The scale on each axis is in miles per hour.

a. Find the speed of the balloon.

b. Find the direction it is traveling relative to east.

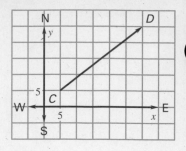

Solution

a. The magnitude of the vector $\overrightarrow{CD}$ represents the balloon's speed. Use the Distance Formula.

$$\left| \overrightarrow{CD} \right| = \underline{\hspace{5cm}} = \underline{\hspace{2cm}} \approx \underline{\hspace{1.5cm}}$$

Answer The speed of the balloon is about ____ miles per hour.

b. The tangent of the angle formed by the vector and a line drawn parallel

to the *x*-axis is ____ , or ____ . Use a

calculator to find the angle measure.

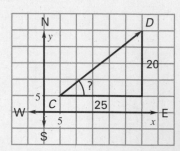

____ 2nd TAN $\approx$ _____ °

Answer The balloon is traveling in a direction about _____° north of east.

✔ **Checkpoint** Complete the following exercise.

1. The vector represents the velocity of a moving hot air balloon. The scale on each axis is in miles per hour. Find the balloon's speed and direction relative to west.

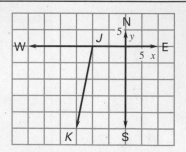

Example 3 *Identifying Equal and Parallel Vectors*

In the diagram, these vectors have the
same direction: _____, _____, ____.

These vectors are equal: _____, ____.

These vectors are parallel:

_____, ____, _____, ___.

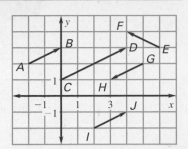

ADDING VECTORS

Sum of Two Vectors

The sum of $\vec{u} = \langle a_1, b_1 \rangle$ and $\vec{v} = \langle a_2, b_2 \rangle$ is

$\vec{u} + \vec{v} = \langle \underline{\quad} + \underline{\quad}, \underline{\quad} + \underline{\quad} \rangle.$

Example 4 *Finding the Sum of Two Vectors*

Let $\vec{u} = \langle 6, -2 \rangle$ and $\vec{v} = \langle -8, 7 \rangle$. Find
the sum $\vec{u} + \vec{v}$.

Solution

To find the sum, add the horizontal
components and add the vertical
components of u and v.

$\vec{u} + \vec{v} = \langle \underline{\quad} + \underline{\quad}, \underline{\quad} + \underline{\quad} \rangle$

$= \langle \underline{\quad}, \underline{\quad} \rangle$

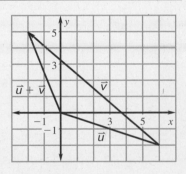

✔ *Checkpoint* Find the sum of the vectors.

2. $\langle 6, 0 \rangle, \langle 1, 3 \rangle$	**3.** $\langle -5, 2 \rangle, \langle 7, -6 \rangle$

Words to Review

Give an example of the vocabulary word.

Pythagorean triple	Special right triangle
Trigonometric ratio	Sine
Cosine	Tangent
Angle of elevation	Solve a right triangle

Magnitude of a vector	Direction of a vector

Equal vectors	Parallel vectors

Sum of two vectors

Review your notes and Chapter 9 by using the Chapter Review on pages 582–584 of your textbook.

10.1 Tangents to Circles

Goals • Identify segments and lines related to circles.
• Use properties of a tangent to a circle.

VOCABULARY

Circle

Radius

Congruent circles

Diameter

Chord

Secant

Tangent

Tangent circles

Concentric

Common tangent

Interior of a circle

Exterior of a circle

Point of tangency

Example 1   *Identifying Special Segments and Lines*

Tell whether the line or segment is best described as a *chord*, a *secant*, a *tangent*, a *diameter*, or a *radius* of ⊙C.

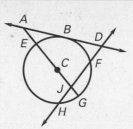

a. $\overline{CG}$ **b.** $\overline{EG}$ **c.** $\overleftrightarrow{AD}$

Solution

a. $\overline{CG}$ is a _____ because C is the center and G is a point on the circle.

b. $\overline{EG}$ is a _____ because it contains the center C.

c. $\overleftrightarrow{AD}$ is a _____ because it intersects the circle at one point.

THEOREM 10.1

If a line is tangent to a circle, then it is perpendicular to the radius drawn to the point of tangency.

    If ℓ is tangent to ⊙Q at P, then __ ⊥ ____.

THEOREM 10.2

In a plane, if a line is perpendicular to a radius of a circle at its endpoint on the circle, then the line is tangent to the circle.

    If ℓ ⊥ $\overline{QP}$ at P, then __ is tangent to ____.

THEOREM 10.3

If two segments from the same exterior point are tangent to a circle, then they are congruent.

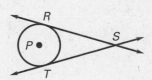

    If $\overleftrightarrow{SR}$ and $\overleftrightarrow{ST}$ are tangent to ⊙P, then

    ____ ≅ ____.

Example 2   *Finding the Radius of a Circle*

You are standing at *R*, 4 feet from a fountain. The distance from you to a point of tangency on the fountain is 8 feet. What is the radius of the fountain?

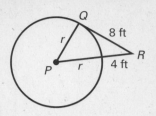

Solution

Tangent $\overleftrightarrow{QR}$ is perpendicular to radius $\overline{PQ}$ at *Q*, so $\triangle PQR$ is a _____. So, you can use the Pythagorean Theorem.

$(r + 4)^2 = r^2 + 8^2$ **Pythagorean Theorem**

$r^2 + 8r + 16 = r^2 + 64$ **Square of binomial**

$8r = $ ___   **Subtract r^2 and 16 from each side.**

$r = $ __   **Divide.**

Answer The radius of the fountain is __ feet.

Example 3   *Using Properties of Tangents*

$\overleftrightarrow{AB}$ is tangent to $\odot C$ at *B*. $\overleftrightarrow{AD}$ is tangent to $\odot C$ at *D*. Find the value of *x*.

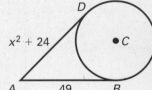

Solution

$AB = AD$ **Use Theorem 10.3.**

___ = _____   **Substitute.**

___ $= x^2$ **Subtract ___ from each side.**

___ $= x$ **Find the square roots of ___.**

✓ **Checkpoint** **Complete the following exercise.**

1. $\overleftrightarrow{AB}$ is tangent to $\odot C$ at *B*. $\overleftrightarrow{AD}$ is tangent to $\odot C$ at *D*. Find the value of *x*.

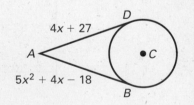

10.2 Arcs and Chords

Goals • Use properties of arcs of circles.
• Use properties of chords of circles.

VOCABULARY

Central angle

Minor arc

Major arc

Semicircle

Measure of a minor arc

Measure of a major arc

Congruent arcs

POSTULATE 26: ARC ADDITION POSTULATE

The measure of an arc formed by two
adjacent arcs is the sum of the measures
of the two arcs.

 $m\overset{\frown}{ABC} =$ _____ + _____

Example 1 *Finding Measures of Arcs*

Find the measure of each arc.

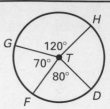

a. $\widehat{DG}$ b. $\widehat{DGH}$ c. $\widehat{DH}$

Solution

a. $m\widehat{DG} = m\widehat{DF} + m\widehat{FG} = \underline{}° + \underline{}° = \underline{}°$

b. $m\widehat{DGH} = m\widehat{DG} + m\widehat{GH} = \underline{}° + \underline{}° = \underline{}°$

c. $m\widehat{DH} = 360° - m\widehat{DGH} = 360° - \underline{}° = \underline{}°$

THEOREM 10.4

In the same circle, or in congruent circles, two minor arcs are congruent if and only if their corresponding chords are congruent.

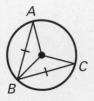

$\widehat{AB} \cong \widehat{BC}$ if and only if $\underline{} \cong \underline{}$.

THEOREM 10.5

If a diameter of a circle is perpendicular to a chord, then the diameter bisects the chord and its arc.

$\overline{DE} \cong \overline{EF},\ \underline{} \cong \underline{}$

THEOREM 10.6

If one chord is a perpendicular bisector of another chord, then the first chord is a diameter.

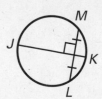

$\underline{}$ is a diameter of the circle.

THEOREM 10.7

In the same circle, or in congruent circles, two chords are congruent if and only if they are equidistant from the center.

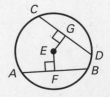

$\overline{AB} \cong \overline{CD}$ if and only if $\underline{} \cong \underline{}$.

Example 2 *Using Theorem 10.5*

Find $m\overparen{KM}$ using Theorem 10.5.

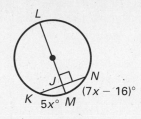

$m\overparen{KM} = m\overparen{MN}$	Theorem 10.5
$5x° = (7x - 16)°$	Substitute.
$\underline{\quad} = \underline{\quad}x - 16$	Subtract $\underline{\quad}$ from each side.
$\underline{\quad} = \underline{\quad}x$	Add $\underline{\quad}$ to each side.
$\underline{\quad} = x$	Divide.

Answer $m\overparen{KM} = 5x° = \underline{\qquad}° = \underline{\quad}°.$

Example 3 *Using Theorem 10.7*

Find QS if $MN = 16$, $RT = 16$, and $NQ = 10$.

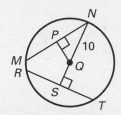

Because $\overline{MN}$ and $\overline{RT}$ are congruent chords, they are equidistant from the center. So, $\overline{PQ} \cong \overline{QS}$. To find QS, first find PN.

$\overline{PQ} \perp \overline{MN}$, so $\overline{PQ}$ bisects $\overline{MN}$. Because $MN = 16$,

$PN = \dfrac{\underline{\qquad}}{\underline{\qquad}} = \underline{\quad}.$

Then use PN to find PQ.

$PN = \underline{\quad}$ and $NQ = 10$, so $\triangle NPQ$ is a $\underline{\quad}$-$\underline{\quad}$-$\underline{\quad}$ right triangle. So, $PQ = \underline{\quad}.$

Finally, use PQ to find QS.

Answer Because $\overline{QS} \cong \overline{PQ}$, $QS = PQ = \underline{\quad}.$

✔ *Checkpoint* Complete the following exercises.

1. Use Theorem 10.5 to find $m\overparen{RS}$. 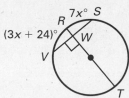	**2.** Find HK if $DG = JL = 24$, and $DH = 13$. 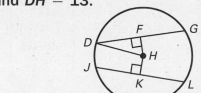

10.3 Inscribed Angles

Goals • Use inscribed angles to solve problems.
• Use properties of inscribed polygons.

VOCABULARY

Inscribed angle

Intercepted arc

Inscribed polygon

Circumscribed circle

THEOREM 10.8: MEASURE OF AN INSCRIBED ANGLE

If an angle is inscribed in a circle, then its measure
is half the measure of its intercepted arc.

$$m\angle ADB = \frac{1}{2}\underline{}$$

THEOREM 10.9

If two inscribed angles of a circle intercept the
same arc, then the angles are congruent.

$$\angle C \cong \angle \underline{}$$

Example 1   *Measures of Arcs and Inscribed Angles*

Find the measure of the arc or angle.

a.

b.

a. $m\angle XYZ = \dfrac{1}{2}$ _____ $= \dfrac{1}{2}$ (____°) = ____°

b. $m\overarc{PQR} = 2m\angle$ _____ $= 2($ ___° $) = $ ____°

Example 2   *Finding the Measure of an Angle*

It is given that $m\angle Y = 62°$. What is $m\angle Z$?

$\angle Y$ and $\angle Z$ both intercept $\overarc{WX}$, so _____ $\cong$ _____.

Answer So, $m\angle$___ $= m\angle$___ $= $ ____°.

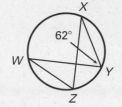

✔ *Checkpoint* Find the measure of the arc or angle.

1. $\angle MNP$	2. $\overarc{RVT}$	3. $\angle A$
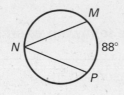	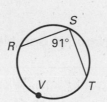	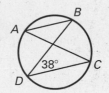

THEOREM 10.10

If a right triangle is inscribed in a circle, then the hypotenuse is a diameter of the circle. Conversely, if one side of an inscribed triangle is a diameter of the circle, then the triangle is a right triangle and the angle opposite the diameter is the right angle.

∠___ is a right angle if and only if _____ is a diameter of the circle.

THEOREM 10.11

A quadrilateral can be inscribed in a circle if and only if its opposite angles are supplementary.

D, E, F, and G lie on some circle, $\odot C$, if and only if $m\angle D + m\angle F = $ _____° and $m\angle E + m\angle G = $ _____°.

Example 3 *Using Theorem 10.10*

Find the value of x.

$\overline{SV}$ is a diameter. So, $\angle T$ is a _____ and $m\angle T = $ ___°.

$15x° = $ ___°

$x = $ __

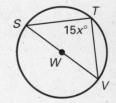

✔ *Checkpoint* **Complete the following exercise.**

4. In the diagram, *WXYZ* is inscribed in $\odot P$. Find the values of *x* and *y*.

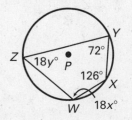

10.4 Other Angle Relationships in Circles

Goals • Use angles formed by tangents and chords to solve problems in geometry.
 • Use angles formed by lines that intersect a circle to solve problems.

THEOREM 10.12

If a tangent and a chord intersect at a point on a circle, then the measure of each angle formed is one half the measure of its intercepted arc.

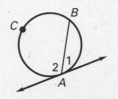

$$m\angle 1 = \frac{1}{2} \underline{\hspace{2cm}}, \qquad m\angle 2 = \frac{1}{2} \underline{\hspace{2cm}}$$

Example 1 *Finding an Angle Measure*

In the diagram below, $\overleftrightarrow{KL}$ is tangent to the circle. Find $m\angle KLM$.

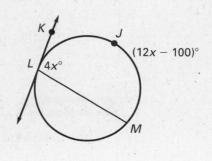

$$m\angle KLM = \underline{\hspace{0.5cm}} \ m\overset{\frown}{MJL}$$

$$4x = \underline{\hspace{0.5cm}} \ (12x - 100)$$

$$\underline{\hspace{0.5cm}} x = 12x - 100$$

$$100 = \underline{\hspace{0.5cm}} x$$

$$\underline{\hspace{0.5cm}} = x$$

Answer $m\angle KLM = (\underline{\hspace{0.5cm}} \cdot \underline{\hspace{0.5cm}})° = \underline{\hspace{0.5cm}}°$

✔ **Checkpoint** Complete the following exercise.

---

1. $\overleftrightarrow{QR}$ is tangent to the circle. Find $m\angle QRS$.

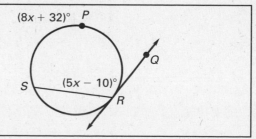

THEOREM 10.13

If two chords intersect in the *interior* of a circle, then the measure of each angle is one half the _____ of the measures of the arcs intercepted by the angle and its vertical angle.

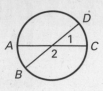

$$m\angle 1 = \frac{1}{2}(m\underline{\quad} + m\underline{\quad}), \, m\angle 2 = \frac{1}{2}(m\underline{\quad} + m\underline{\quad})$$

THEOREM 10.14

If a tangent and a secant, two tangents, or two secants intersect in the *exterior* of a circle, then the measure of the angle formed is one half the _____ of the measures of the intercepted arcs.

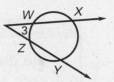

$$m\angle 1 = \frac{1}{2}(m\underline{\quad} - m\underline{\quad})$$

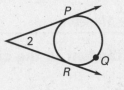

$$m\angle 2 = \frac{1}{2}(m\underline{\quad} - m\underline{\quad})$$

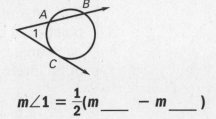

$$m\angle 3 = \frac{1}{2}(m\underline{\quad} - m\underline{\quad})$$

Example 2   *Measure of an Angle Formed by Two Chords*

Find the value of x.

Solution

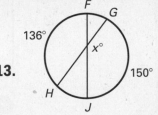

$$x° = \frac{1}{2}(m\underline{\quad} + m\underline{\quad}) \quad \textbf{Apply Theorem 10.13.}$$

$$x° = \frac{1}{2}(\underline{\quad}° + \underline{\quad}°) \quad \textbf{Substitute.}$$

$$x = \underline{\quad} \quad\quad\quad\quad \textbf{Simplify.}$$

Example 3   *Using Theorem 10.14*

Find the value of *x*.

a.
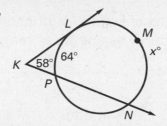

b.
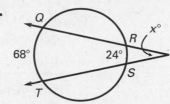

Solution

a. $m\angle LKP = \frac{1}{2}(m\widehat{LMN} - m\widehat{LP})$ **Apply Theorem 10.14.**

  $\underline{\quad}° = \frac{1}{2}(x° - \underline{\quad}°)$ **Substitute.**

  $\underline{\quad\quad} = x - \underline{\quad\quad}$ **Multiply each side by 2.**

  $\underline{\quad\quad} = x$ **Solve for *x*.**

b. $x = \frac{1}{2}(m\widehat{QT} - m\widehat{RS})$ **Apply Theorem 10.14.**

  $= \frac{1}{2}(\underline{\quad} - \underline{\quad})$ **Substitute.**

  $= \frac{1}{2}(\underline{\quad})$ **Subtract.**

  $= \underline{\quad}$ **Multiply.**

✔ *Checkpoint* **Find the value of *x*.**

2.
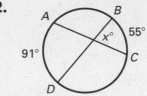

3.
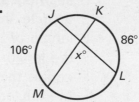

4.
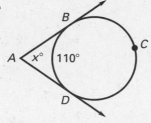

5.
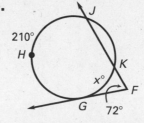

10.5 Segment Lengths in Circles

Goals • Find the lengths of segments of chords.
• Find the lengths of segments of tangents and secants.

THEOREM 10.15

If two chords intersect in the interior of a circle, then the product of the lengths of the segments of one chord is equal to the product of the lengths of the segments of the other chord.

$$EA \cdot \underline{\hspace{1cm}} = EC \cdot \underline{\hspace{1cm}}$$

THEOREM 10.16

If two secant segments share the same endpoint outside a circle, then the product of the length of one secant segment and the length of its external segment equals the product of the length of the other secant segment and the length of its external segment.

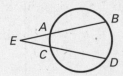

$$EA \cdot \underline{\hspace{1cm}} = EC \cdot \underline{\hspace{1cm}}$$

THEOREM 10.17

If a secant segment and a tangent segment share an endpoint outside a circle, then the product of the length of the secant segment and the length of its external segment equals the square of the length of the tangent segment.

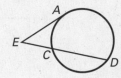

$$(\underline{\hspace{1cm}})^2 = EC \cdot ED$$

Example 1 *Finding Segment Lengths*

Chords $\overline{JN}$ and $\overline{KM}$ intersect inside the circle.
Find the value of x.

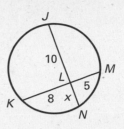

$LJ \cdot LN =$ ___ · ___   Theorem _____

$10 \cdot x =$ ___ · ___   Substitute.

$10x =$ ___   Simplify.

$x =$ ___   Divide each side by 10.

Example 2 *Finding Segment Lengths*

Find the value of x.

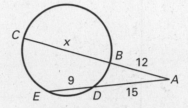

Solution

$AB \cdot AC = AD \cdot AE$ Theorem _____

___ · $(x +$ ___ $) = 15 \cdot ($ ___ $+$ ___ $)$ Substitute.

___ $x +$ ___ = ___   Simplify.

$x =$ ___   Solve for x.

Example 3 *Estimating the Radius of a Circle*

You are standing at a point Q, about
9 feet from a large circular tent. The
distance from you to a point of tangency
on the tent is about 24 feet. Estimate the
radius of the tent.

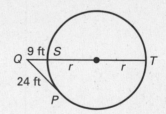

Solution

$(QP)^2 = QS \cdot QT$ Use Theorem _____.

___$^2 \approx 9 \cdot ($ ___ $r +$ ___ $)$ Substitute.

___ $\approx$ ___ $r +$ ___   Simplify.

___ $\approx$ ___ r Subtract ___ from each side.

___ $\approx r$ Divide each side by ___.

Answer So, the radius of the tent is about ___ feet.

Example 4   *Finding Segment Lengths*

Use the figure at the right to find
the value of *x*.

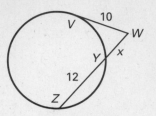

$$(\underline{\qquad})^2 = WY \cdot \underline{\qquad}$$ **Theorem 10.17**

$$\underline{\qquad}^2 = x \cdot (\underline{\qquad} + \underline{\qquad})$$ **Substitute.**

$$0 = \underline{\qquad}^2 + \underline{\qquad} - \underline{\qquad}$$ **Write in standard form.**

$$x = \frac{-\underline{\qquad} \pm \sqrt{\underline{\qquad}^2 - 4(1)(\underline{\qquad})}}{2}$$ **Use Quadratic Formula.**

$$x = \underline{\qquad} \pm \underline{\qquad}$$ **Simplify.**

Use the positive solution, because lengths cannot be negative.

Answer So, $x =$ _____ + _____ ≈ _____ .

✓ *Checkpoint* Complete the following exercises.

1. Chords $\overline{MP}$ and $\overline{NQ}$ intersect inside the circle. Find the value of *x*. 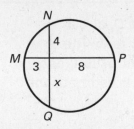	**2.** Find the value of *x*. 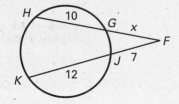

3. Find the value of *x*.

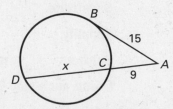

10.6 Equations of Circles

Goals • Write the equation of a circle.
• Use the equation of a circle and its graph to solve problems.

VOCABULARY

Standard equation of a circle:

Example 1   *Writing a Standard Equation of a Circle*

Write the standard equation of the circle with center (0, 6) and radius 3.6.

$$(x - h)^2 + (y - k)^2 = r^2$$ **Standard equation of a circle**

$$(x - \underline{})^2 + (y - \underline{})^2 = \underline{}^2$$ **Substitute.**

$$x^2 + (y - \underline{})^2 = \underline{}$$ **Simplify.**

Example 2   *Writing a Standard Equation of a Circle*

The point (−1, 1) is on a circle whose center is (−3, 4). Write the standard equation of the circle.

Find the radius. The radius is the distance from the point (−1, 1) to the center (−3, 4).

$$r = \sqrt{(-3 - (\underline{}))^2 + (\underline{} - 1)^2}$$ **Use the Distance Formula.**

$$r = \sqrt{(\underline{})^2 + \underline{}^2}$$ **Simplify.**

$$r = \sqrt{\underline{}}$$ **Simplify.**

Substitute $(h, k) = (-3, 4)$ and $r = \underline{}$ into the standard equation of a circle.

$$(x - (\underline{}))^2 + (y - \underline{})^2 = (\underline{})^2$$ **Standard equation of a circle**

$$(x + \underline{})^2 + (y - \underline{})^2 = \underline{}$$ **Simplify.**

Example 3 *Graphing a Circle*

The equation of a circle is $(x - 3)^2 + (y + 1)^2 = 16$. Graph the circle.

Rewrite the equation to find the center and radius:

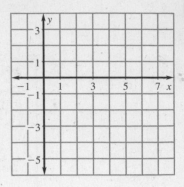

$$(x - 3)^2 + (y + 1)^2 = 16$$

$$(x - 3)^2 + [y - (\underline{})]^2 = \underline{}^2$$

The center is (__, ____) and the radius is __. To graph the circle, place the point of a compass at (__, ____), set the radius at __ units, and swing the compass to draw a full circle.

✔ *Checkpoint* Complete the following exercises.

1. Write the standard equation of a circle with center $(-5, -3)$ and radius 5.2.

2. The point $(4, -5)$ is on a circle whose center is $(-2, 3)$. Write the standard equation of the circle.

3. Graph the equation $(x - 1)^2 + (y + 3)^2 = 9$.

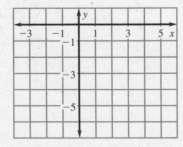

Example 4 *Applying Graphs of Circles*

Skydiving A skydiving instruction school has a field with multiple landing targets. Each target is circle shaped. A coordinate plane is used to arrange the targets in the field, with the corner of the field as the origin. The equation $(x - 8)^2 + (y - 4)^2 = 9$ represents one of the targets.

a. Graph the landing target.

b. The landing spots by the following skydivers are located as follows: Marika is at (7, 3), Alex is at (3, 4), Julia is at (10, 7), and Caleb is at (9, 6). Which skydivers landed on the target?

Solution

a. Rewrite the equation to find the center and radius:

$$(x - 8)^2 + (y - 4)^2 = 9$$
$$(x - 8)^2 + (y - 4)^2 = \underline{}^2$$

The center is (__, __) and the radius is __. Graph the circle below.

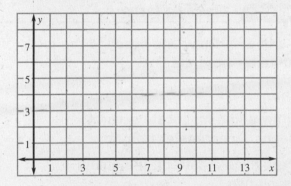

b. Graph the landing spots of the skydivers. The graph shows that _____ and _____ both landed on the target.

10.7 Locus

Goals • Draw the locus of points that satisfy a given condition.
• Draw the locus of points that satisfy two or more conditions.

VOCABULARY

Locus

Example 1   *Finding a Locus*

Draw a line *m*. Draw and describe the locus of all points that are 1 centimeter from the line.

Solution

1. Draw a line *m*. Locate several points 1 centimeter from *m*.

2. Recognize a pattern: the points lie on two _____.

3. Draw the _____.

Answer The locus of points that are 1 centimeter from *m* are two _____ to *m*.

✔ **Checkpoint** Complete the following exercise.

1. Describe the locus of points equidistant from the vertices of an equilateral equiangular triangle.

Example 2 **A Locus Satisfying Two Conditions**

Lines *c* and *d* are in a plane. What is the locus of points in the plane that are equidistant from *c* and *d* and within *x* units from the origin?

Solution

The locus of all points that are equidistant from *c* and *d* are the lines $x =$ ___ and $y =$ ___.

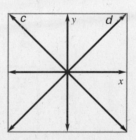

The locus of all points that are a distance of *x* units from *c* and *d* is a _____ centered at the _____ with a _____ of *x*.

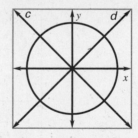

The intersection of the loci, or locus points, are the line segments from (___, ___) to (___, ___) and (___, ___) to (___, ___).

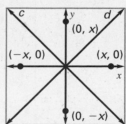

Example 3 **A Locus Satisfying Three Conditions**

Points R(2, 4), S(6, 4), and T(7, 4) lie in a plane. What is the locus of points in the plane equidistant from R and S, 2 units from R and 3 units from T?

Solution

The locus of points equidistant from R and S is the _____

_____ of $\overline{RS}$. The locus of points 2 units from R is a _____.
The locus of points 3 units from T is a _____. Draw the _____
and _____ in the coordinate plane.

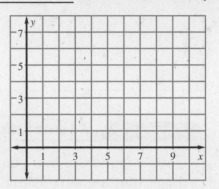

Answer The locus is at (__ , __).

✔ **Checkpoint** Complete the following exercises.

2. Points V and W lie in a plane. What is the locus of points
   3 centimeters from V and equidistant from V and W?

---

3. Three circles with centers at (2, 2),
   (6, 2), and (4, 4) each have a radius
   of 2 units. Draw the locus of points
   and find the point of intersection of
   the three circles.

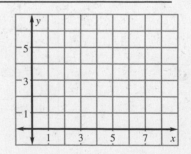

Words to Review

Give an example of the vocabulary word.

Center, radius, diameter of circle	**Congruent circles**
Chord, secant, tangent	**Tangent circles**
Concentric circles	**Common tangents**
Interior of a circle	**Exterior of a circle**
Point of tangency	**Central angle**

Minor arc, major arc	Semicircle
Congruent arcs	Inscribed angle, intercepted arc
Inscribed polygon	Circumscribed circle
Tangent segment, secant segment	External segment
Standard equation of a circle	Locus

Review your notes and Chapter 10 by using the Chapter Review on pages 650–652 of your textbook.

Angle Measures in Polygons

Goals • Find the measures of interior and exterior angles of polygons.
• Use measures of angles of polygons to solve problems.

THEOREM 11.1: POLYGON INTERIOR ANGLES THEOREM

The sum of the measures of the interior angles of a convex *n*-gon is

$(n - \underline{}) \cdot \underline{}°.$

COROLLARY TO THEOREM 11.1

The measure of each interior angle of a regular *n*-gon is

$\dfrac{1}{\boxed{}} \cdot (n - \underline{}) \cdot \underline{}°,$ or $\dfrac{\left(n - \boxed{}\right) \cdot \boxed{}}{\boxed{}}.$

Example 1 *Finding Measures of Interior Angles of Polygons*

Find the value of *x* in the diagram.

Solution

The sum of the measures of the interior angles of any pentagon is
$(\underline{} - \underline{}) \cdot \underline{}° = \underline{} \cdot \underline{}° = \underline{}°.$

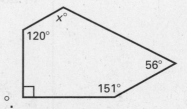

Add the measures of the interior angles of the pentagon.

$120° + 90° + 151° + 56° + x° = \underline{}°$ The sum is \underline{}°.

$\underline{} + x = \underline{}$ Simplify.

$x = \underline{}$ Subtract \underline{} from each side.

Answer The measure of the fifth interior angle of the pentagon is \underline{}°.

THEOREM 11.2: POLYGON EXTERIOR ANGLES THEOREM

The sum of the measures of the exterior angles of a convex polygon, one angle at each vertex, is _____°.

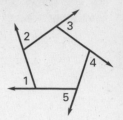

COROLLARY TO THEOREM 11.2

The measure of each exterior angle of a regular *n*-gon is

$$\frac{1}{\boxed{}} \cdot \underline{}°, \text{ or } \frac{\boxed{}}{\boxed{}}.$$

Example 2 — Finding the Measure of an Exterior Angle

Find the value of *x*.

a.

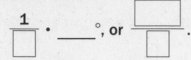

b.

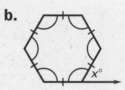

Solution

a. $90° + x° + 2x° + 32° + (2x - 12)° = $ _____°   Use Theorem 11.2.

$5x + $ _____ $= $ _____   Simplify.

$5x = $ _____   Subtract.

$x = $ _____   Divide.

b. $x° = \dfrac{1}{\boxed{}} \cdot \underline{}°$ Use $n = $ ___ in the Corollary to Theorem 11.2.

$= $ _____   Simplify.

✔ *Checkpoint* Find the value of *x*.

1.

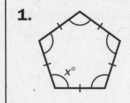

2.

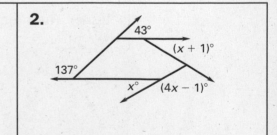

Example 3 *Finding Angle Measures of a Polygon*

Rugs The rug shown at the right contains a hexagonal design. Four of the angles in the hexagon have a measure of 150°. The other two angles are congruent. What is the measure of each angle?

Solution

Draw a sketch	The diagram shows a sketch of the design. The design is a nonregular hexagon. $\angle B$, $\angle C$, $\angle E$, and $\angle F$ each measure _____°, and $\angle A$ is congruent to $\angle$___. The sum of the measures of the interior angles of the hexagon is _____°.

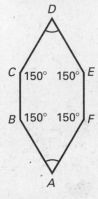

Verbal Model

Sum of measures of interior angles	=	___ •	Measure of each obtuse angle	+

___ •	Measure of $\angle A$ and $\angle D$

Labels   Sum of measures of interior angles = _____ (degrees)

Measure of each obtuse angle = _____ (degrees)

Measure of $\angle A$ and $\angle D = x$ (degrees)

Reasoning   _____ = ___ • _____ + 2x   Write an equation.

_____ = _____ + 2x   Simplify.

_____ = 2x   Subtract _____ from each side.

_____ = x   Divide each side by 2.

Answer The measure of each of the two congruent angles is ___°.

11.2 Areas of Rectangular Polygons

Goals • Find the area of an equilateral triangle.
• Find the area of a regular polygon.

VOCABULARY

Center of a polygon

Radius of a polygon

Apothem of a polygon

Central angle of a regular polygon

THEOREM 11.3: AREA OF AN EQUILATERAL TRIANGLE

The area of an equilateral triangle is
one fourth the square of the length
of the side times _____.

A = _____

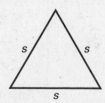

Example 1 *Finding the Area of an Equilateral Triangle*

Find the area of an equilateral triangle with 12 inch sides.

Solution

Use $s = 12$ in the formula from Theorem 11.3.

$$A = \frac{1}{4}\sqrt{3}s^2 = \frac{1}{4}\sqrt{3}(\underline{\quad}^2) = \frac{1}{4}(\underline{\quad})\sqrt{3} = \underline{\quad} \text{ in.}^2$$

Answer The area is _____ square inches, or about _____ square inches.

✓ *Checkpoint* Find the area of the triangle.

1.
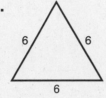

2.

$4\sqrt{7}$

THEOREM 11.4: AREA OF A REGULAR POLYGON

The area of a regular *n*-gon with side length *s* is half the product of the apothem *a* and the perimeter *P*.

$$A = \frac{1}{2}\underline{\quad} \quad \text{or} \quad A = \frac{1}{2}\underline{\quad} \cdot \underline{\quad}$$

Example 2 *Finding the Area of a Regular Polygon*

A regular octagon is inscribed in a circle with radius 1 unit. Find the area of the octagon.

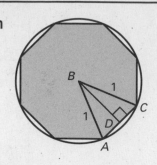

Solution

To apply the formula for the area of a regular octagon, find its apothem and perimeter.

The measure of central $\angle ABC$ is ____°.

In isosceles triangle $\triangle ABC$, the altitude BD bisects $\angle$_____ and side ____ . So, $m\angle DBC =$ _____°. In right triangle $\triangle BDC$, you can use trigonometric ratios to find the lengths of the legs.

To find the measure of the central angle of a regular polygon, divide 360° by its number of sides.

$$\cos \underline{\quad}° = \frac{BD}{\boxed{}} = \frac{BD}{\boxed{}} = \underline{\quad}$$

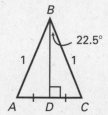

$$\sin \underline{\quad}° = \frac{CD}{\boxed{}} = \frac{CD}{\boxed{}} = \underline{\quad}$$

So, the apothem is $a = BD =$ _____.

The perimeter is $P = 8(\underline{\quad}) = 8(2 \cdot \underline{\quad}) =$ _____.

The area of the octagon is

$$A = \frac{1}{2}\underline{\quad} = \frac{1}{2}(\underline{\qquad})(\underline{\qquad}) \approx \underline{\quad}.$$

Answer The area of the octagon is about ____ square units.

✔ **Checkpoint** Find the area of the regular polygon.

3.

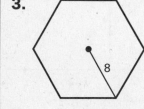

4.

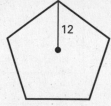

Perimeters and Areas of Similar Figures

Goals • Compare perimeters and areas of similar figures.
• Use perimeters and areas of similar figures to solve real-life problems.

THEOREM 11.5: AREAS OF SIMILAR POLYGONS

If two polygons are similar with the lengths of corresponding sides in the ratio of $a:b$, then the ratio of their areas is ___ : ___.

$$\frac{\text{Side length of Quad. I}}{\text{Side length of Quad. II}} = \underline{\quad}$$

$$\frac{\text{Area of Quad. I}}{\text{Area of Quad. II}} = \underline{\quad}$$

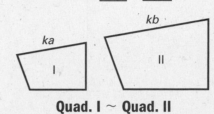

Quad. I ~ Quad. II

Example 1   *Finding Ratios of Similar Polygons*

Hexagons A and B are similar.

a. Find the ratio (unshaded to shaded) of the perimeters of the hexagons.

b. Find the ratio (unshaded to shaded) of the areas of the hexagons.

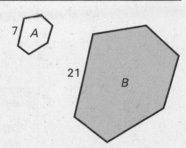

Solution

The ratio of the lengths of corresponding sides in the hexagons is

$\dfrac{}{} = \dfrac{}{}$, or __ : __.

a. The ratio of the perimeters is also __ : __. So, the perimeter of hexagon A is _____ the perimeter of hexagon B.

b. Using Theorem 11.5, the ratio of the area is ___ : ___, or __ : __. So, the area of hexagon A is _____ the area of hexagon B.

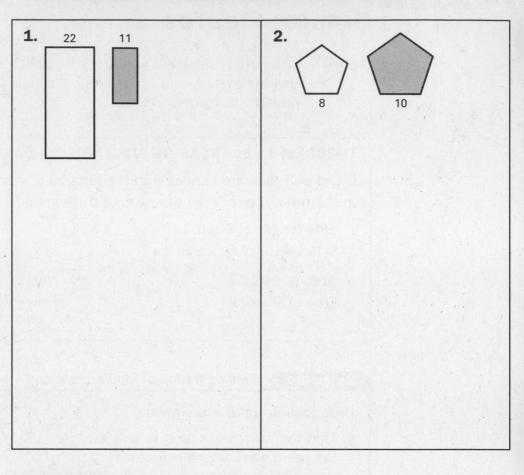

1.   22   11

2.   8   10

Example 2   *Using Areas of Similar Figures*

Comparing Costs You want to carpet a room that measures 40 feet by 48 feet. An advertisement states that the cost to carpet a room that measures 10 feet by 12 feet is $216. What is a reasonable cost for the larger room?

Solution

The ratio of the lengths of corresponding sides are equal. The ratio of the side lengths is 1: ___. So, the ratio of the areas is 1^2: ___, or 1: ___.

Because the cost of the carpet should be a function of its area, the carpet for the larger room should cost about _____ times that of the smaller room.

___ × **216** = _____

Answer A reasonable cost for the larger room is $_____.

Example 3 *Finding Perimeters and Areas of Similar Polygons*

Gazebos A park has two gazebos. The floor of each gazebo has the shape of a regular hexagon. The floor of one gazebo has a perimeter of 72 feet and an area of about 374.12 square feet. The floor of the larger gazebo has a perimeter of 96 feet. Find its area.

Solution

All regular hexagons are similar because all corresponding angles are congruent and the corresponding side lengths are proportional.

Find the ratio of the perimeters of the two gazebos. This ratio is the same as the ratio of their side lengths.

$$\frac{\text{Perimeter of smaller gazebo}}{\text{Perimeter of larger gazebo}} = \frac{72}{\boxed{}} = \underline{}$$

Calculate the area of the larger gazebo. Let *A* represent the area of the larger gazebo. The ratio of the area of the smaller gazebo to the area of the larger gazebo is __^{2} : __^{2}, or __ : __.

$$\underline{} = \frac{\boxed{}}{A}$$ Write proportion.

__ • *A* = __(_____)   Cross product property

A = _____   Divide each side by __.

A ≈ _____   Use a calculator.

Answer The area of the larger gazebo is about _____ square feet.

✓ **Checkpoint** Complete the following exercise.

3. In Example 3, assume that the floor of the larger gazebo has a perimeter of 120 feet. Find its area.

11.4 Circumference and Arc Length

Goals • Find the circumference of a circle and the length of a circular arc.
• Use circumference and arc length to solve problems.

VOCABULARY

Circumference

Arc length

THEOREM 11.6: CIRCUMFERENCE OF A CIRCLE

The circumference C of a circle is $C = $ _____ or $C = $ _____, where d is the diameter of the circle and r is the radius of the circle.

Example 1 *Using Circumference*

a. Find the circumference of a circle with radius 9 inches.

b. Find the diameter of a circle with a circumference of 58 inches.

Solution

a. $C = 2\pi r$

$= 2 \cdot \pi \cdot$ ___

$= $ ___ π

$\approx$ _____

So, the circumference is about _____ inches.

b. $C = \pi d$

___ $= \pi d$

$\dfrac{\boxed{}}{\pi} = d$

_____ $\approx d$

So, the diameter is about _____ inches.

✔ *Checkpoint* Find the indicated measure.

1. Circumference	2. Radius
25 cm	$C = 70$ ft

ARC LENGTH COROLLARY

In a circle, the ratio of the length of a given arc to the circumference is equal to the ratio of the measure of the arc to 360°.

$$\frac{\text{Arc length of } \widehat{AB}}{\boxed{}} = \frac{m\widehat{AB}}{\boxed{}}, \text{ or}$$

$$\text{Arc length of } \widehat{AB} = \frac{m\widehat{AB}}{\boxed{}} \cdot \underline{}$$

Example 2 *Finding Arc Lengths*

Find the length of each arc.

a. 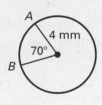   b. 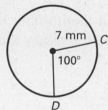   c.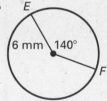

Solution

a. Arc length of $\widehat{AB} = \underline{} \cdot 2\pi(\underline{\ }) \approx \underline{}$ millimeters

b. Arc length of $\widehat{CD} = \underline{} \cdot 2\pi(\underline{\ }) \approx \underline{}$ millimeters

c. Arc length of $\widehat{EF} = \underline{} \cdot 2\pi(\underline{\ }) \approx \underline{}$ millimeters

✔ **Checkpoint** Find the indicated measure.

3. Length of $\overset{\frown}{AB}$

4. Length of $\overset{\frown}{MN}$

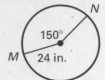

Example 3 **Using Circumference**

Tricycles The diagram at the right shows two tires from a tricycle. How many revolutions does each tire make while traveling 250 feet? Round answers to one decimal place.

20 in.   16 in.

Solution

The larger tire has a diameter of ____ inches. Its circumference is π • ____, or about _____ inches.

The smaller tire has a diameter of ____ inches. Its circumference is π • ____, or about _____ inches.

To find the number of revolutions made, divide the distance the tricycle travels by the tire circumference.

Larger tire: $\dfrac{250 \text{ ft}}{\boxed{} \text{ in.}} = \dfrac{\boxed{} \text{ in.}}{\boxed{} \text{ in.}}$ **Convert feet to inches.**

$\approx$ _____   **Simplify.**

Smaller tire: $\dfrac{250 \text{ ft}}{\boxed{} \text{ in.}} = \dfrac{\boxed{} \text{ in.}}{\boxed{} \text{ in.}}$ **Convert feet to inches.**

$\approx$ _____   **Simplify.**

Answer The larger tire makes about _____ revolutions in 250 feet and the smaller tire makes about _____ revolutions in 250 feet.

11.5 Areas of Circles and Sectors

Goals • Find the area of a circle and a sector of a circle.
• Use areas of circles and sectors to solve problems.

VOCABULARY

Sector of a circle

THEOREM 11.7: AREA OF A CIRCLE

The area of a circle is π times the square
of the radius.

$A =$ _____

Example 1 *Using the Area of a Circle*

a. Find the area of ⊙P.

b. Find the diameter of ⊙Q.

Area = 125 in.²

Solution

a. Use $r =$ ____ in the area
formula.

$A = \pi r^2$

$= \pi \cdot$ ___ ^{2}

$=$ ____ π

$\approx$ _____

The area is ____ π, or about
_____, square centimeters.

b. The diameter is _____
the radius.

$A = \pi r^2$

____ $= \pi r^2$

$\dfrac{\boxed{}}{\pi} = r^2$

_____ $\approx r^2$

____ $\approx r$

The diameter is about
__(____), or _____, inches.

1. Area	**2.** Area	**3.** Diameter
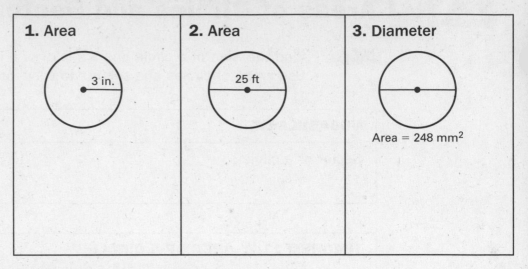 3 in.	25 ft	Area = 248 mm²

THEOREM 11.8: AREA OF A SECTOR

The ratio of the area A of a sector of a circle to the area of the circle is equal to the ratio of the measure of the intercepted arc to 360°.

$$\frac{A}{\boxed{}} = \frac{\boxed{}}{360°}, \text{ or } A = \frac{\boxed{}}{360°} \cdot \underline{}$$

Example 2 *Finding the Area of a Sector*

Find the area of the sector.

Solution

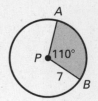

Sector *APB* intercepts an arc whose measure is _____.

The radius is ___ units.

$$A = \frac{\boxed{}}{360°} \cdot \underline{}$$ **Formula for area of a sector**

$$= \frac{\boxed{}}{360°} \cdot \pi(\underline{}^2)$$ **Substitute known values.**

$$\approx \underline{}$$ **Use a calculator.**

Answer The area of the sector is about _____ square units.

✓ **Checkpoint** Find the area of the shaded region.

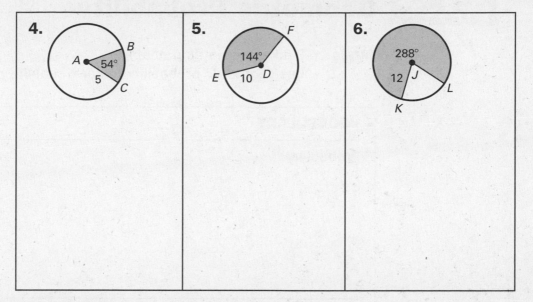

4.	5.	6.

Example 3 *Finding the Area of a Region*

Find the area of the shaded region.

Solution

The shaded region consists of a rectangle and two sectors of a circle.

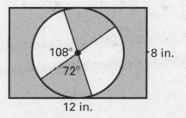

The rectangle has a length of ____ inches and a width of ___ inches. The radius of the circle is ___ inches.

$$\boxed{\text{Area}} = \boxed{\begin{array}{c}\text{Area of}\\\text{rectangle}\end{array}} - 2 \cdot \boxed{\begin{array}{c}\text{Area of one}\\\text{unshaded sector}\end{array}}$$

$$= \underline{\quad} \cdot \underline{\quad} - 2 \cdot \frac{\boxed{}}{360°} \cdot \pi \cdot \underline{\quad}^2$$

$$= \underline{\quad} - 2\left(\frac{\boxed{}}{10} \cdot \pi \cdot \underline{\quad}\right)$$

$$= \underline{\quad} - \frac{\boxed{}}{5}\pi$$

$$\approx \underline{\qquad}$$

Answer The area of the shaded region is about _____ square inches.

11.6 Geometric Probability

Goals • Find a geometric probability.
• Use geometric probability to solve real-life problems.

VOCABULARY

Probability

Geometric probability

GEOMETRIC PROBABILITY

Probability and Length

Let $\overline{AB}$ be a segment that contains the segment $\overline{CD}$. If a point K on $\overline{AB}$ is chosen at random, then the probability that K is on $\overline{CD}$ is

$$P(\text{Point } K \text{ is on } \overline{CD}) = \underline{\hspace{3cm}}.$$

Probability and Area

Let J be a region that contains region M. If a point K in J is chosen at random, then the probability that K is in region M is

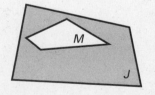

$$P(\text{Point } K \text{ is in region } M) = \underline{\hspace{3cm}}.$$

Example 1   *Finding a Geometric Probability*

Find the probability that a point chosen at random on $\overline{PQ}$ is on $\overline{RS}$.

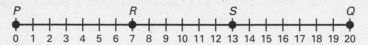

Solution

$P(\text{Point is on } \overline{RS}) = \dfrac{\text{Length of } \boxed{}}{\text{Length of } \boxed{}} = \underline{} = \underline{}$

> You can write a probability as a fraction, as a decimal, or as a percent.

Answer The probability can be written as $\underline{}$, $\underline{}$, or $\underline{}$.

Example 2   *Using Areas to Find a Geometric Probability*

Golf A golf ball is hit and lands on the circular green shown. The ball is equally likely to land on any point on the green. Find the probability that the ball lands in the cup.

Solution

Convert the radius of the green to inches. Then find the ratio of the area of the hole to the area of the golf green.

$30 \text{ ft} = \underline{} \text{ in.}$ **Convert feet to inches.**

$P(\text{Ball lands in cup}) = \dfrac{\text{Area of cup}}{\text{Area of green}}$ **Write ratio.**

$= \dfrac{}{}$ **Formula for area of circle**

$= \dfrac{}{}$ **Divide out common factor.**

$\approx \underline{}$ **Use a calculator.**

Answer The probability that the ball lands in the cup is about $\underline{}$.

1. Find the probability that a point chosen at random on $\overline{AB}$ is on $\overline{CD}$.

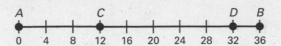

The area of a trapezoid is

$$A = \frac{1}{2}h(b_1 + b_2)$$

where h is the height of the trapezoid and b_1 and b_2 are the lengths of the bases.

2. Find the probability that a randomly chosen point in the figure lies in the shaded region.

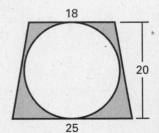

3. You are expecting a visit from a friend anytime between 3:00 P.M. and 5:00 P.M. During this time, you know that you will need to spend 20 minutes cleaning your room. What is the probability that your friend will arrive while you are cleaning your room?

Words to Review

Give an example of the vocabulary word.

Center of a polygon	Radius of a polygon
Apothem of a polygon	Central angle of a regular polygon
Circumference	Arc length
Sector of a circle	Geometric probability

Review your notes and Chapter 11 by using the Chapter Review on pages 708–710 of your textbook.

12.1 Exploring Solids

Goals • Use properties of polyhedra.
• Use Euler's Theorem.

VOCABULARY

Polyhedron

Face

Edge

Vertex

Regular polyhedron

Convex polyhedron

Cross section

Platonic solids

Tetrahedron

Octahedron

Dodecahedron

Icosahedron

TYPES OF SOLIDS

Of the five solids below, the prism and pyramid are polyhedra.
The cylinder, sphere, and cone are not polyhedra.

Prism   Cylinder   Pyramid   Sphere   Cone

Example 1   *Identifying Polyhedra*

Decide whether the solid is a polyhedron. If so, count the number of
faces, vertices, and edges of the polyhedron.

a. 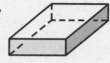   b. 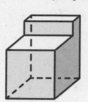   c.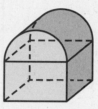

Solution

a. This is a polyhedron. It has ___ faces, ___ vertices, and
   ____ edges.

b. This is a polyhedron. It has ___ faces, ____ vertices, and
   ___ edges.

c. This is not a polyhedron. Some of the faces are not polygons.

Example 2   *Classifying Polyhedra*

Is the polyhedron convex? Is it regular?

a. 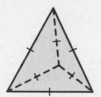   b.   c.

_____   _____   _____

THEOREM 12.1: EULER'S THEOREM

The number of faces (*F*), vertices (*V*), and edges (*E*) of a polyhedron are related by the formula $F + V = E +$ ___.

Example 3 — Using Euler's Theorem

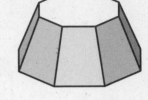

The solid has 10 faces: 8 trapezoids and 2 octagons. How many vertices does the solid have?

On their own, 8 trapezoids and 2 octagons have 8(___) + 2(___) = ___ sides. In the solid, each side is shared by exactly two polygons. So the number of edges is ___. Use Euler's Theorem to find the number of vertices.

$$F + V = E + 2 \qquad \text{Write Euler's Theorem.}$$
$$\underline{\quad} + V = \underline{\quad} + 2 \qquad \text{Substitute.}$$
$$V = \underline{\quad} \qquad \text{Solve for } V.$$

Answer The solid has ___ vertices.

✔ **Checkpoint** Is the solid a polyhedron? If so, is it convex? Is it regular?

1.	2.	3.

4. **Critical Thinking** Is it possible for a polyhedron to have 16 faces, 34 vertices, and 50 edges? Explain.

12.2 Surface Area of Prisms and Cylinders

Goal • Find the surface area of a prism and of a cylinder.

VOCABULARY

Prism

Right prism

Oblique prisms

Surface area of a polyhedron

Lateral area of a polyhedron

Net

Cylinder

Right cylinder

Lateral area of a cylinder

Surface area of a cylinder

THEOREM 12.2: SURFACE AREA OF A RIGHT PRISM

The surface area S of a right prism can be found using the
formula $S = 2B +$ _____ , where B is the area of a base, P is the
perimeter of a base, and h is the height.

Example 1   *Using Theorem 12.2*

Find the surface area of the right prism.

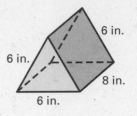

Solution

Each base is an equilateral triangle with a side
length, s, of ___ inches. Using the formula for the
area of an equilateral triangle, the area of each
base is

$$B = \frac{1}{4}\sqrt{3}(s^2) = \frac{1}{4}\sqrt{3}(\_\_^2) = \_\_\sqrt{3} \text{ in.}^2$$

The perimeter of each base is $P =$ ____ in.
and the height is $h =$ ___ in.

Answer So, the surface area is

$$S = 2B + Ph = 2(\_\_\sqrt{3}) + \_\_\_(\_\_) \approx \_\_\_\_ \text{ in.}^2$$

✔ **Checkpoint** Find the surface area of the right prism.

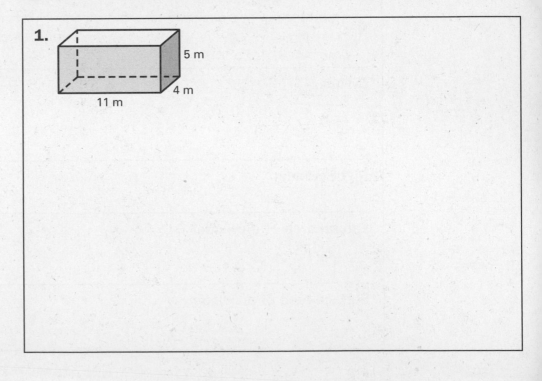

1.

THEOREM 12.3: SURFACE AREA OF A RIGHT CYLINDER

The surface area S of a right cylinder is

$S = 2B + Ch = $ _____,

where B is the area of a base, C is the
circumference of a base, r is the radius
of a base, and h is the height.

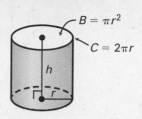

Example 2 *Finding the Surface Area of a Cylinder*

Find the surface area of the right cylinder.

Solution

Each base has a radius of ___ meters,
and the cylinder has a height of ___ meters.

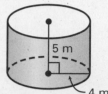

$S = 2\pi r^2 + 2\pi rh$ **Formula for surface area of a cylinder**

$= 2\pi(\_\_)^2 + 2\pi(\_\_)(\_\_)$ **Substitute.**

$= \_\_\_\pi + \_\_\_\pi$ **Simplify.**

$= \_\_\_\pi$ **Add.**

$\approx$ _____   **Use a calculator.**

Answer The surface area is about _____ square meters.

✔ **Checkpoint** Find the surface area of the right cylinder. Round
your result to two decimal places.

2.

9 ft

6 ft

Surface Area of Pyramids and Cones

Goal • Find the surface area of a pyramid and of a cone.

VOCABULARY

Pyramid

Regular pyramid

Circular cone or cone

Right cone

Lateral surface of a cone

Example 1   *Finding the Area of a Lateral Face*

> A *regular pyramid* is considered a regular polyhedron only if *all* its faces, including the base, are congruent. So, the only pyramid that is a regular polyhedron is the regular triangular pyramid, or *tetrahedron*.

Find the area of each lateral face of the regular pyramid shown at the right.

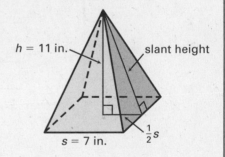

$h = 97$ m

slant height

$s = 90$ m

$\frac{1}{2}s$

Solution

To find the slant height of the pyramid, use the Pythagorean Theorem.

$(\text{Slant height})^2 = h^2 + \left(\frac{1}{2}s\right)^2$ **Write formula.**

$(\text{Slant height})^2 = \underline{\quad}^2 + \underline{\quad}^2$ **Substitute.**

$(\text{Slant height})^2 = \underline{\qquad}$ **Simplify.**

$\text{Slant height} = \underline{\qquad}$ **Take the positive square root.**

$\text{Slant height} \approx \underline{\qquad}$ **Use a calculator.**

Answer So, the area of each lateral face is

$\frac{1}{2}$(base of lateral face)(slant height), or about $\frac{1}{2}$(____)(_____),

which is about _____ square meters.

✓ *Checkpoint* Complete the following exercise.

1. Find the area of a lateral face of the regular pyramid. Round the result to one decimal place.

$h = 11$ in.

slant height

$s = 7$ in.

$\frac{1}{2}s$

THEOREM 12.4: SURFACE AREA OF A REGULAR PYRAMID

The surface area S of a regular pyramid is $S = B +$ _____ , where

B is the area of the base, P is the perimeter of the base, and l is the slant height.

Example 2 *Finding the Surface Area of a Pyramid*

To find the surface area of the regular pyramid shown, start by finding the area of the base.

Use the formula for the area of a regular polygon, $\frac{1}{2}$(apothem)(perimeter).

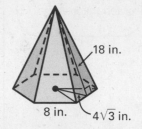

A diagram of the base is shown at the right. After substituting, the area of the base is $\frac{1}{2}(4\sqrt{3})(6 \cdot$ ___), or ___ $\sqrt{3}$ square inches.

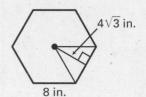

Now you can find the surface area, using ___ $\sqrt{3}$ for the area of the base, B.

$S = B + \dfrac{1}{2}Pl$ **Write formula.**

$= \underline{} \sqrt{3} + \dfrac{1}{2}(\underline{})(\underline{})$ **Substitute.**

$= \underline{} \sqrt{3} + \underline{}$ **Simplify.**

$\approx \underline{}$ **Use a calculator.**

Answer So, the surface area is about _____ square inches.

THEOREM 12.5: SURFACE AREA OF A RIGHT CONE

The surface area S of a right cone is

$$S = \pi r^2 + \underline{\hspace{1cm}},$$

where r is the radius of the base and l is the slant height.

Example 3 *Finding the Surface Area of a Right Cone*

To find the surface area of the right cone shown, use the formula for the surface area.

$S = \pi r^2 + \pi r l$	**Write formula.**
$= \pi(\underline{\hspace{0.5cm}})^2 + \pi(\underline{\hspace{0.5cm}})(\underline{\hspace{0.5cm}})$	**Substitute.**
$= \underline{\hspace{0.5cm}} \pi + \underline{\hspace{0.5cm}} \pi$	**Simplify.**
$= \underline{\hspace{0.5cm}} \pi$	**Add.**

Answer The surface area is ____ π square meters, or about
_____ square meters.

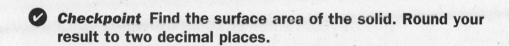

✓ **Checkpoint** Find the surface area of the solid. Round your result to two decimal places.

2. Regular pyramid	**3.** Right cone
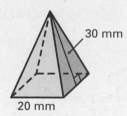	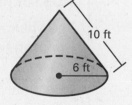

12.4 Volume of Prisms and Cylinders

Goals • Use volume postulates.
• Find the volumes of prisms and cylinders.

VOCABULARY

Volume of a solid

POSTULATE 27: VOLUME OF A CUBE

The volume of a cube is the cube of the length of its side, or
$V =$ ___ .

POSTULATE 28: VOLUME CONGRUENCE POSTULATE

If two polyhedra are congruent, then _____
_____ .

POSTULATE 29: VOLUME ADDITION POSTULATE

The volume of a solid is the _____ of the volumes of all its
nonoverlapping parts.

THEOREM 12.6: CAVALIERI'S PRINCIPLE

If two solids have the same height and the same cross-sectional
area at every level, then they have the same _____ .

THEOREM 12.7: VOLUME OF A PRISM

The volume V of a prism is $V =$ ____ , where B is the area of a
base and h is the height.

THEOREM 12.8: VOLUME OF A CYLINDER

The volume V of a cylinder is $V = Bh =$ _____ , where B is the
area of a base, h is the height, and r is the radius of a base.

Example 1 *Finding Volumes*

Find the volume of the right prism and the right cylinder.

a.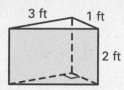
3 ft   1 ft

2 ft

b.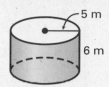
5 m

6 m

Solution

a. The area B of the base is $\frac{1}{2}$(__)(__), or ___ ft^2. Use $h = 2$ to find the volume.

$V = Bh =$ ___ (__) = __ ft^3

b. The area B of the base is $\pi \cdot$ __^{2}, or ___π m^2. Use $h = 6$ to find the volume.

$V = Bh =$ ___$\pi($__$) =$ ___$\pi \approx$ _____ m^3

✓ *Checkpoint* **Find the volume of the solid. Round your result to two decimal places.**

1. Right prism	2. Right cylinder
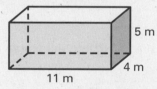 5 m 4 m 11 m	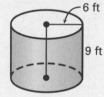 6 ft 9 ft

Example 2   *Using Volumes*

Use the measurements given to solve for *x*.

a. Cube,
  V = 90 ft^3

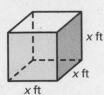

b. Right cylinder,
  V = 1253 m^3

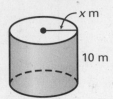

Solution

a. A side length of the cube is *x* feet.

$$V = s^3 \qquad \text{Formula for volume of cube}$$

$$\underline{\quad} = x^3 \qquad \text{Substitute.}$$

$$\underline{\qquad} \approx x \qquad \text{Take the cube root.}$$

Answer So, the height, width, and length of the cube are about
  $\underline{\qquad}$ feet.

b. The area of the base is πx^2 square meters.

$$V = Bh \qquad\qquad \text{Formula for volume of cylinder}$$

$$\underline{\qquad} = \pi x^2(\underline{\quad}) \qquad \text{Substitute.}$$

$$\underline{\qquad} = \underline{\quad}\pi x^2 \qquad \text{Rewrite.}$$

$$\frac{\boxed{}}{\boxed{}\,\pi} = x^2 \qquad \text{Divide each side by } \underline{\quad}\,\pi.$$

$$\underline{\qquad} \approx x^2 \qquad \text{Simplify.}$$

$$\underline{\qquad} \approx x \qquad \text{Find the positive square root.}$$

Answer So, the radius of the cylinder is about $\underline{\qquad}$ meters.

12.5 Volume of Pyramids and Cones

Goal • Find the volume of pyramids and cones.

THEOREM 12.9: VOLUME OF A PYRAMID

The volume V of a pyramid is $V =$ _____ , where

B is the area of the base and h is the height.

THEOREM 12.10: VOLUME OF A CONE

The volume V of a cone is $V =$ _____ = _____ ,

where B is the area of the base, h is the height, and
r is the radius of the base.

Example 1   *Finding the Volume of a Pyramid*

Find the volume of the pyramid with the
regular base.

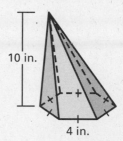

10 in.

4 in.

Solution

The base can be divided into six equilateral
triangles. Using the formula for the area of an

equilateral triangle, $\frac{1}{4}\sqrt{3} \cdot s^2$, the area of the

base B can be found as follows:

$$\underline{\quad} \cdot \frac{1}{4}\sqrt{3} \cdot s^2 = \underline{\quad} \cdot \frac{1}{4}\sqrt{3} \cdot \underline{\quad}^2 = \underline{\quad}\sqrt{3} \text{ in.}^2$$

4 in.

Use Theorem 12.9 to find the volume of the pyramid.

$$V = \frac{1}{3}Bh = \frac{1}{3}(\underline{\qquad})(\underline{\quad}) = \underline{\quad}\sqrt{3}$$

Answer The volume of the pyramid is ____ $\sqrt{3}$, or about
_____ cubic inches.

Example 2 *Finding the Volume of a Cone*

Find the volume of each cone.

a. Right circular cone

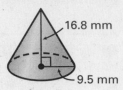

16.8 mm

9.5 mm

b. Oblique circular cone

12 ft

4.5 ft

Solution

a. Use the formula for the volume of a cone.

$$V = \frac{1}{3}Bh \qquad \text{Formula for volume of cone}$$

$$= \frac{1}{3}(\pi r^2)h \qquad \text{Base area equals } \pi r^2.$$

$$= \frac{1}{3}(\pi \underline{\quad}^2)\underline{\quad} \qquad \text{Substitute.}$$

$$= \underline{\quad}\pi \qquad \text{Simplify.}$$

Answer The volume of the cone is _____ π, or about _____ cubic millimeters.

b. Use the formula for the volume of a cone.

$$V = \frac{1}{3}Bh \qquad \text{Formula for volume of cone}$$

$$= \frac{1}{3}(\pi r^2)h \qquad \text{Base area equals } \pi r^2.$$

$$= \frac{1}{3}(\pi \underline{\quad}^2)\underline{\quad} \qquad \text{Substitute.}$$

$$= \underline{\quad}\pi \qquad \text{Simplify.}$$

Answer The volume of the cone is ___ π, or about _____ cubic feet.

Checkpoint Find the volume of the solid. Round your result to two decimal places.

1. Pyramid with regular base	2. Right circular cone
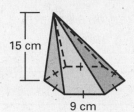 15 cm 9 cm	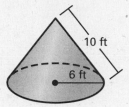 10 ft 6 ft

---

Example 3   *Using the Volume of a Cone*

Use the given measurements to solve for *x*.

Solution

$$V = \frac{1}{3}(\pi r^2)h \qquad \text{Formula for volume}$$

$$\underline{\quad\quad} = \frac{1}{3}(\pi x^2)(\underline{\quad}) \qquad \text{Substitute.}$$

$$\underline{\quad\quad} = \underline{\quad}\pi x^2 \qquad \text{Multiply each side by } \underline{\quad}.$$

$$\underline{\quad\quad\quad} \approx x^2 \qquad \text{Divide each side by } \underline{\quad}.$$

$$\underline{\quad\quad\quad} \approx x \qquad \text{Find positive square root.}$$

8 m

x

Volume = 135 m³

Answer The radius of the cone is about _____ meters.

Surface Area and Volume of Spheres

Goals • Find the surface area of a sphere.
• Find the volume of a sphere.

VOCABULARY

Sphere

_____

Radius of a sphere

_____

Chord of a sphere

_____

Diameter of a sphere

_____

Great circle

_____

Hemisphere

THEOREM 12.11: SURFACE AREA OF A SPHERE

The surface area S of a sphere with radius r is $S =$ _____.

Example 1 **Finding the Surface Area of a Sphere**

Find the surface area. When the radius doubles, does the surface area double?

a. 3 cm

b. 6 cm

Solution

a. $S = 4\pi r^2 = 4\pi(\underline{})^2 = \underline{}\pi$ cm^2

b. $S = 4\pi r^2 = 4\pi(\underline{})^2 = \underline{}\pi$ cm^2

The surface area of the sphere in part (b) is _____ times greater than the surface area of the sphere in part (a) because

____ $\pi \cdot$ ___ = ____ π.

Answer When the radius of a sphere doubles, the surface area

_____.

Example 2 **Using a Great Circle**

The circumference of a great circle of a sphere is 7.4π feet. What is the surface area of the sphere?

Solution

Begin by finding the radius of the sphere.

$C = 2\pi r$ **Formula for circumference of circle**

_____ $= 2\pi r$ **Substitute for C.**

_____ $= r$ **Divide each side by 2π.**

Using a radius of ____ feet, the surface area is

$S = 4\pi r^2 = 4\pi(\underline{})^2 = \underline{}\pi$ ft^2.

Answer The surface area of the sphere is _____ π ft^2, or about

____ ft^2.

THEOREM 12.12: VOLUME OF A SPHERE

The volume V of a sphere with radius r is $V = \underline{}$.

Example 3 *Finding the Volume of a Sphere*

What is the radius of a sphere made from the cylinder of modeling clay shown? Assume the sphere has the same volume as the cylinder.

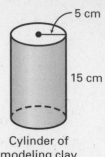

Cylinder of modeling clay

Solution

To find the volume of the cylinder of modeling clay, use the formula for the volume of a cylinder.

$$V = \pi r^2 h = \pi(\underline{\hspace{0.5cm}})^2(\underline{\hspace{0.5cm}}) = \underline{\hspace{0.8cm}} \pi \text{ cm}^3$$

To find the radius of the sphere, use the formula for the volume of a sphere and solve for *r*.

Sphere made from cylinder of modeling clay

$$V = \frac{4}{3}\pi r^3 \qquad \text{Formula for volume of sphere}$$

$$\underline{\hspace{0.8cm}}\pi = \frac{4}{3}\pi r^3 \qquad \text{Substitute for } V.$$

$$\underline{\hspace{0.8cm}}\pi = 4\pi r^3 \qquad \text{Multiply each side by } \underline{\hspace{0.3cm}}.$$

$$\underline{\hspace{1.2cm}} = r^3 \qquad \text{Divide each side by } \underline{\hspace{0.4cm}}.$$

$$\underline{\hspace{0.8cm}} \approx r \qquad \text{Use a calculator to take the cube root.}$$

Answer The radius of the sphere is about _____ centimeters.

✔ *Checkpoint* Find the surface area and volume of the sphere. Round your results to two decimal places.

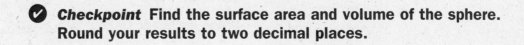

1.  5 ft	**2.** 6.5 m

Similar Solids

Goals • Find and use the scale factor of similar solids.
• Use similar solids to solve real-life problems.

VOCABULARY

Similar solids

Example 1 *Identifying Similar Solids*

Decide whether the two solids are similar. If so, compare the volumes of the solids.

a.   b.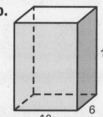

Solution

a. The solids are not similar because the ratios of corresponding linear measures are not equal, as shown.

   lengths: ___   widths: ___   heights: ___ ___ =

b. The solids are similar because the ratios of corresponding linear measures are equal, as shown. The solids have a scale factor of __ : __.

   lengths: ___ ___ =   widths: ___ ___ =   heights: ___ ___ =

The volume of the larger prism is $V = Bh =$ ____(___) = ____.

The volume of the smaller prism is $V = Bh =$ ____(___) = ____.

The ratio of side lengths is __ : __ and the ratio of volumes is ____ : ____ , or __ : __.

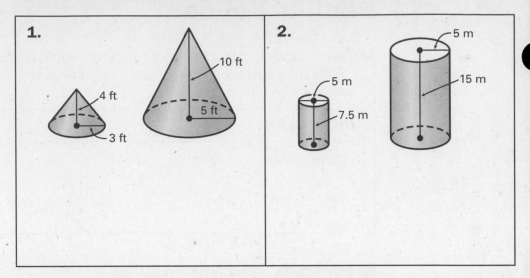

Checkpoint Decide whether the two solids are similar.

1.

2.

THEOREM 12.13: SIMILAR SOLIDS THEOREM

If two similar solids have a scale factor of $a:b$, then corresponding areas have a ratio of ___:___, and corresponding volumes have a ratio of ___:___.

Example 2   *Using the Scale Factor of Similar Solids*

Cylinders A and B are similar with a scale factor of $2:5$. Find the surface area and volume of cylinder B given that the surface area of cylinder A is 96π square feet and the volume of cylinder A is 128π cubic feet.

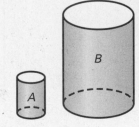

Solution

Begin by using Theorem 12.13 to set up two proportions.

$$\frac{\text{Surface area of } A}{\text{Surface area of } B} = \frac{}{\underline{\hspace{1cm}}} \qquad \frac{\text{Volume of } A}{\text{Volume of } B} = \frac{}{\underline{\hspace{1cm}}}$$

$$\frac{96\pi}{\text{Surface area of } B} = \frac{}{\underline{\hspace{1cm}}} \qquad \frac{128\pi}{\text{Volume of } B} = \frac{}{\underline{\hspace{1cm}}}$$

Surface area of B = _____   Volume of B = _____

Answer The surface area of cylinder B is _____ square feet and the volume of cylinder B is _____ cubic feet.

Example 3 **Finding the Scale Factor of Similar Solids**

The two cones are similar. Find the scale factor.

$V = 108\pi$ cm^3

$V = 256\pi$ cm^3

Solution

Find the ratio of the two volumes.

$\dfrac{a^3}{b^3} = \dfrac{108\pi}{256\pi}$ **Write ratio of volumes.**

$\dfrac{a^3}{b^3} = $ ____   **Simplify.**

$\dfrac{a}{b} = $ ____   **Find the cube root.**

Answer The two cones have a scale factor of __ : __ .

Example 4 **Comparing Similar Solids**

Two punch bowls are similar with a scale factor of 2 : 3. The amount of concentrate to be added is proportional to the volume. How much concentrate does the smaller bowl require if the larger bowl requires 48 ounces?

Solution

Using the scale factor, the ratio of the volume of the smaller punch bowl to the larger punch bowl is

$$\dfrac{a^3}{b^3} = \dfrac{\boxed{}^3}{\boxed{}^3} = \underline{} \approx \dfrac{1}{\boxed{}}.$$

The ratio of the volumes of the concentrates is about 1 : ____ . The amount of concentrate for the smaller punch bowl can be found by multiplying the amount of concentrate for the larger punch bowl by

$\dfrac{1}{\boxed{}}$ as follows: ____ $\left(\dfrac{1}{\boxed{}}\right) \approx$ ____ ounces.

Answer The smaller bowl requires about ____ ounces of concentrate.

Words to Review

Give an example of the vocabulary word.

Polyhedron, face, edge, vertex	Convex, regular polyhedron
Platonic solid	Tetrahedron
Prism, bases, lateral faces	Right prism
Oblique prism	Surface area of a polyhedron

Right cylinder	Surface area of a cylinder
Regular pyramid	Right circular cone, lateral surface
Volume of a solid	Sphere, center, radius
Sphere, chord, diameter	Great circle
Similar solids	

Review your notes and Chapter 12 by using the Chapter Review on pages 774–776 of your textbook.